A Guide to
Assertive
Training

ACHIEVING ASSERTIVE BEHAVIOR

ACHIEVING ASSERTIVE BEHAVIOR

A Guide to Assertive Training

Harold H. Dawley, Jr.

*Veterans Administration Hospital,
New Orleans and
Tulane University
School of Medicine*

W. W. Wenrich

*North Texas
State University*

BROOKS/COLE PUBLISHING COMPANY
Monterey, California

A Division of Wadsworth Publishing Company, Inc.

To Linda, Robert, and Michael
(H. H. D.)

To Kevin Drew Wenrich
(W. W. W.)

BF
575
A85D38

ISBN: 0-8185-0185-5
L.C. Catalog Card No.: 76-19915
Printed in the United States of America

10 9 8 7 6 5 4 3 2 1

Production Editor: *Fiorella Ljunggren*
Interior & Cover Design: *John Edeen*

FOREWORD

When I first wrote about assertive training, in 1949, I hoped that it would someday become an accepted form of therapy. Since that time a great deal of research has been done on the subject. This book surveys that research with unobtrusive thoroughness. I'm sure that anyone who reads this excellent book will find the experience highly rewarding.

Andrew Salter

Preface

This book was written for people who are concerned with the development of *assertive behavior*, or the ability to secure and maintain one's rights while respecting the rights of others. Assertive behavior, as such, involves the accurate expression of one's thoughts and feelings in a frank and open manner.

The style and basic approach of this book are rather informal and represent our attempt to present the behavioral techniques and procedures of assertive training in a clear, concise, and readily comprehensible manner. Although oriented toward the student in the behavioral sciences and "helping" professions, such as psychology, psychiatry, social work, rehabilitation, counseling, education, nursing, speech pathology, and related professional and paraprofessional fields, this book is also intended to be of direct value to the individual concerned with the development of his or her own assertive behavior. Thus the materials contained herein should serve in large measure as a "self-help" guide. Additionally, we hope that many therapists will find the book useful as they engage in helping their clients pursue more effective assertive behavior.

The orientation of this book is that of behavior therapy, an approach based on general psychology with an emphasis on learning. However, with the possible exception of Chapter Six ("Behavioral Procedures"), the book has not been written with the same terminological rigor and consistency that one would expect to find in an exposition of behavior-therapy/behavior-modification techniques. We have permitted a greater degree of "license" in our discussion of assertive training for two reasons: first, the audience for which our book is aimed is a much less limited one than that addressed by most behavior-therapy texts, and, second, the somewhat more "expansive" and popular terminology we have employed should enhance the comprehension and practical application of assertive-training procedures for this rather wide audience. Nevertheless, in Chapter Two most of the basic principles and terms used in behavior therapy are discussed, and references are provided for the reader interested in a more extensive account of these ideas.

Part One of this book focuses on the background and development of assertive training. A general overview of the topic is provided in Chapter One.

Chapter Two briefly describes the principles of behavior, the ways in which behavior is acquired, maintained, and modified, and the basic principles of operant conditioning—a method of predicting and controlling behavior. The chapter also discusses the evolution of behavior therapy, particularly assertive training. The general nature of adaptive and unadaptive behavior is covered in Chapter Three, where assertive behavior is presented as an adaptive style of interaction, with nonassertiveness and aggressiveness presented as unadaptive styles.

Part Two of this book describes the practical application of assertive training. Chapter Four stresses the importance of behavioral analysis, which involves identifying the unadaptive target behavior and preparing to replace it with more appropriate assertive behavior, and of the correct evaluation of one's behavior. Chapter Five presents a fairly detailed coverage of verbal assertive behavior—such as speaking loudly enough to be heard, talking about oneself, and initiating, maintaining, and terminating conversations—as well as assertive nonverbal behavior—such as maintaining the appropriate physical distance when interacting with other people and the postural stance, facial expressions, and other nonverbal behaviors that denote an assertive person. Chapter Six is somewhat more technically oriented and discusses the major behavioral procedures for developing assertive behavior, including behavioral rehearsal, role playing, modeling, the practiced expression of emotions, and the use of covert conditioning techniques and reinforcement. Some experimental research relating to the application of these procedures is also presented. Chapter Seven deals with the pitfalls and difficulties commonly encountered in trying to develop assertiveness and provides a summary statement regarding the maintenance of assertive behavior.

Detailed muscle-relaxation exercises are provided in Appendix A. The purpose of these exercises is to help the individual achieve a state of complete muscle relaxation. Appendix B provides several copies of the Assertive Behavior Record Form—a useful device for identifying and recording one's responses and thus gaining a better understanding of the areas of one's behavior that need to become more assertive.

Thanks and appreciation are extended to our colleagues Thomas Gilbride, Lawrence S. Guidry, George S. Greenberg, Craig Maumus, Lou Moffett, Chester B. Scrignor, and Cecil (Woody) Wingfield for their thoughtful suggestions and criticisms during the preparation of this manuscript. We would also like to acknowledge the assistance of the other reviewers who read and commented on the manuscript: Stephen T. Carey of the University of Alberta, Virginia M. Coplan of Applied Potential, Jean C. DiLeo of New Orleans Public Schools, Richard M. Eisler of the Veterans Administration's Psychology Service in Jackson, Mississippi, Victor Halling of Bakersfield College, Alan E. Kazdin of Pennsylvania State University, Joseph E. Morrow of California State University at Sacramento, Bernice Podel of California State University at Chico, Andrew Salter, and Raymond W. Swan of Tulane University.

Special thanks are also extended to Claire Verduin and Fiorella Ljung-gren of Brooks/Cole for their untiring efforts in seeing this book through to its present form.

Harold H. Dawley, Jr.
W. W. Wenrich

Contents

Nonassertiveness: A case study   *xv*

Part One: Background and development   1

Chapter One: General overview   *3*

Chapter Two: Principles of behavior and the development of assertive training as a behavior therapy   *6*
    Topic overview   *6*
    Respondent and operant behavior   *7*
    Basic concepts and terminology of operant conditioning   *8*
    Behavior therapy   *10*
    The rise of assertive training   *11*
    Suggested readings   *13*

Chapter Three: Adaptive versus unadaptive behavior   *15*
    Topic overview   *15*
    Assertiveness as adaptive behavior and nonassertiveness as unadaptive behavior   *17*
    Nonassertiveness   *19*
    Aggressiveness   *23*

Part Two: Practical applications   31

Chapter Four: Preparing for assertive training   *33*
    Topic overview   *33*
    Behavioral analysis   *34*
    How to correctly evaluate one's behavior   *43*
    Reality testing   *44*
    Cognitive restructuring   *45*
    Suggested reading   *47*

Chapter Five: Assertive verbal and nonverbal behavior   *48*
    Topic overview   48
    Assertive verbal behavior   49
    Assertive nonverbal behavior   61

Chapter Six: Behavioral procedures   64
    Topic overview   64
    Developing verbal skills   65
    Developing nonverbal skills   67
    Behavioral rehearsal and role playing   67
    Modeling   70
    Covert conditioning techniques   77
    The use of reinforcement   80
    Information giving, coaching, and homework   83
    Use of video- and audiotapes   83
    Relaxation training   85
    *Positive assertion and situational determinants of assertive
        behavior   86*
    Use of the Assertive Behavior Record Form   88
    Suggested readings   89

Chapter Seven: Troubleshooting   91
    Topic overview   91
    Crisis situations   92
    Dealing with someone who tries to make you feel guilty   92
    ''Impossible'' people   93
    When assertion does not work   94
    Choosing not to assert yourself   97
    Temporary aggressiveness during assertive training   98
    Recovery after a fall   99
    Maintaining assertive behavior   99

References   101

Appendix A: Muscle relaxation exercises   105

Appendix B: Assertive Behavior Record Form   111

Index   117

A Guide to Assertive Training

ACHIEVING ASSERTIVE BEHAVIOR

Nonassertiveness: A case study

For as long as Bob can remember, he has always experienced a sinking sensation in the pit of his stomach and felt the other discomforting sensations associated with fear and anxiety whenever he encounters situations that call for assertive responses. He is a tall, handsome, rather rugged-looking individual and has many charming and appealing characteristics. But because of his defensive facade, all that most people see are his habitual unadaptive, ineffectual, and generally unappealing responses to social situations that he cannot cope with effectively.

A particularly difficult and at times even terrifying social interaction for Bob involves having to deal with someone while other people are present, such as when waiting to be served at a busy counter with many other customers clamoring for service. Instead of clearly attracting the attention of the salesclerk when it is his turn to be waited on, he lingers in the background, fearful of raising his voice or of being conspicuous. He stands there feeling nervous and foolish until the clerk finally asks him what he needs. With a great deal of anxiety, and many times with an equal degree of confusion, he blurts out his request. Any questions by the clerk in an attempt to clarify his order are perceived by Bob as being a put-down. He feels extremely self-conscious and will generally say whatever he can to quickly terminate the transaction. He leaves these situations red-faced and humiliated—and often without getting exactly what he came for.

Bob is a moderately successful draftsman and, being fairly conscientious, has favorably impressed his supervisors. On many of the projects on which he works, various parts are assigned to different people in his office. A recurring problem for Bob for nearly the entire two years that he has been with this firm has been the tendency of a few of the other employees to slough off some of their work onto him. Bob does not want to do other people's work but has been unable to say so. On the contrary, when they mockingly bring up the point that he does some of their tasks, he laughs it off, saying that he really doesn't mind. But he does mind, and the problem eats away at him physiologically and psychologically whenever it occurs. He feels a great deal of resentment and hostility toward his coworkers as a result but, unfortunately, is unable to convey these feelings to them.

There are a few people with whom Bob feels completely at ease and who can therefore recognize and appreciate his individuality. However, most people perceive him as a quiet, shy, tense, and even standoffish individual who apparently does not have any strong feelings about anything, since he seldom, if ever, takes stands on issues and hardly ever says no, regardless of how unreasonable a request may be. He is seen as "straight" in the sense that he lacks spontaneity and as distant in that he never expresses his true feelings. What Bob feels around people is apprehension, which they also pick up and feel.

This picture of Bob represents what you will see identified in this book as a nonassertive individual—someone who has not learned to assert himself or herself and has instead developed ways of responding that are ineffective and that produce anxiety and other discomforts.

Fortunately, Bob sought out professional assistance from someone proficient in the behavior-therapy techniques referred to as assertive training. After several sessions spent in clearly identifying his problem, he was exposed to some of the treatments you will see discussed in this book. Within a reasonably short time he found that he could confidently attract the attention of clerks and be served promptly. He was also able to effectively discuss with his coworkers his feelings about doing more than his share of work and tactfully but assertively rectified that problem. He has changed from a timid, anxious individual to one who feels relatively at ease in social situations. He enjoys the self-respect that comes from standing up for his rights. All is not perfect with Bob (or, indeed, with most of the rest of us). But he has made a major behavioral change that has significantly improved his life. It is hoped that this exposure to assertive training will likewise help you to change your own behavior or to assist others who are in need of behavioral change.

Part One / Background and development

Chapter One / *General overview*

    To achieve an understanding of assertiveness, we should view behavior as occurring on a continuum. At one end are negative traits such as phoniness, excessive inhibition, hypocrisy, deception, aggressiveness, hostility, debilitating anxiety, and similar unadaptive, self-defeating behaviors; at the other end are the more positive, adaptive characteristics, such as emotional honesty, effective communication, self-respect, and respect for others, all of which are associated with appropriate assertiveness. Assertive individuals do not try to offend or alienate people. On the contrary, their assertive behavior is intended to result in (among other things) decreased anxiety and hostility, increased interpersonal understanding, and the ability to establish close and meaningful relationships. In general, assertive behavior should improve the overall quality of social interactions as well as enhance one's personal esteem.

    Traditional psychotherapy—by which we mean nonbehaviorally oriented psychotherapy—has long been characterized by the use of nonbehavioral procedures for treating behavior disorders. Personal problems, such as an irrational fear of heights or an inability to say no to unreasonable demands, are considered to be "symptoms." They are a consequence of intrapsychic conflict, with the unadaptive behavior viewed as resulting from internal repressed or underlying factors. The therapist tries to help the individual resolve these inner conflicts by developing "insight" or understanding regarding their origin. This goal is brought about primarily by the individual's talking while the therapist listens and "interprets" (giving his or her conception of the meaning of what the individual is saying). When the repressed material has been brought to a conscious level, the conflict that previously resulted in the appearance of symptoms disappears and, theoretically, the problem is solved. Unfortunately, however, there is much evidence to suggest that, conceptually and practically, this has not been the case (as will be seen in Chapter Six). The fact that most of the nonbehavioral therapists have emphasized talking and little more was articulately stressed some time ago by Ford and Urban (1963) in their textbook on psychotherapy. They maintained:

> Although the other therapists [discussed in that volume] have developed somewhat different ways of thinking about behavior disorders, they all use fundamentally the same treatment approach. They sit and talk with the patient. They differ in the content they believe should be discussed, as well as when and how to discuss it, but they do not propose the extensive use of other procedures [pp. 273–274].

Behavior therapists, on the other hand, view unadaptive behaviors as instances of faulty or inappropriate learning, and treatment is designed to replace these inadequate response patterns with adaptive behaviors. This treatment utilizes empirically developed strategies, techniques, and procedures. "Talking" is recognized as important, but the behavior therapist uses it to produce a change in the client's *behavior* rather than to achieve conflict resolution. In discussing the behavior therapist's emphasis on studying behavior, Deibert and Harmon (1972) state:

> What we really refer to when we speak of "personality" are the behaviors we see a person performing. We don't see a "personality"; we merely observe a person's behaviors. In the case of our college wallflower [a case cited earlier in their text], we did not see "introvert" stamped on her anywhere. We couldn't cut her brain open and find a lump of introversion. We did, however, observe her behavior (how frequently she dated boys, how frequently she engaged in social activities, how frequently she talked with people, how frequently she smiled, etc.) and then lumped all these behaviors together under the label of "introvert" [p. 5].

In general, then, we can say that learning does not occupy a central role in traditional psychotherapy, whereas it is the core of behavior therapy. However, this distinction is becoming increasingly less clear-cut. Although not necessarily identified as such, the development of assertive behaviors frequently becomes a technique and goal in most psychotherapeutic and related processes, since one of the primary aims of psychotherapeutic endeavors is to assist individuals in becoming more open, emotionally honest, and able to express feelings in appropriate manners—in essence, by our definition, in becoming more assertive.

In recent years behavior therapy in general and (to a lesser degree) assertive training in particular have been attracting increasing attention. Professionals of many persuasions are coming to accept the behavioral approach with its conceptualizations and focus on the remediation of unadaptive behavior. The success and application of assertive training have been demonstrated in primary and secondary schools, in clinics and hospitals, and in a large number of other settings involving interpersonal interaction. Assertive training can be of value to the teacher, parent, pastor, youth leader, marriage counselor, psychologist, social worker, psychiatrist, nurse, speech pathologist, and rehabilitation counselor—as well as to any individual interested in improving his or her own social skills.

Principles of behavior and the development of assertive training as a behavior therapy

Chapter Two

Topic Overview

I. Respondent and operant behavior
   1. Respondent behavior is a reaction of the organism to the environment; it is elicited by a stimulus and is controlled by the autonomic nervous system.
   2. Operant behavior is an action of the organism on the environment; it is emitted (rather than elicited) and is controlled by the central nervous system.

II. Operant conditioning
   1. Operant conditioning is a method of predicting and controlling behavior, based on the principle that rewarding consequences (reinforcers) strengthen behavior.
   2. Positive reinforcers strengthen behavior by being added to the situation.
   3. Negative reinforcers strengthen behavior by being withdrawn from the situation.
   4. Behavior can be eliminated by either punishment or nonreinforcement.
   5. Punishment decreases the probability of a behavior by presenting an aversive event when the behavior occurs.
   6. Extinction is the elimination of a behavior through nonreinforcement.
   7. Intermittent reinforcement (reinforcement administered only part of the time) increases resistance to extinction.

III. Behavior therapy

   1. Behavior therapy is a type of therapy that seeks to modify unadaptive behavior by applying general principles of psychology and by employing empirically developed strategies and procedures, with an emphasis on learning principles and techniques.

   2. Behavior therapy entails a certain amount of "art" but is supported by the rigorously scientific substratum of continuing experimental research.

IV. Assertive training

   1. Assertive training is a major type of behavior therapy designed to develop assertive behavior.

   2. It can be effective in the treatment of a wide variety of problems relating to moderate-to-severe deficits in social interactional skills.

   3. It operates on the premise that, while some individuals are not assertive because of excessive inhibition, others simply have not learned how to assert themselves.

Respondent and Operant Behavior

For nearly two decades there has been a great deal of interest in the application of conditioning principles to the modification of human behaviors. Novels with this theme sell widely; academic and professional societies with this orientation flourish; texts and professional journals in this domain are published at an exceptionally high rate. This chapter is intended to familiarize you with these principles and with the general manner in which they are currently being applied, together with other procedures, in a rather specific, and very important, area of human activity: the development of assertive behavior.

For purposes of prediction and control, psychologists find it useful to distinguish two types of behavior: respondent and operant. A *respondent* behavior is a *reaction* of the organism *to* the environment—an involuntary, elicited, automatic response controlled by the autonomic nervous system. The presentation of the *eliciting stimulus* is all that is usually required for the occurrence of the response. Examples of respondent behavior are salivating when a lemon drop is placed in your mouth, "tearing" when a grain of sand is caught in your eye, and "startling" when you hear a loud, unanticipated noise. Respondent behavior is involved in anger, guilt, fear, anxiety, and all the other uncomfortable and sometimes incapacitating emotional responses that frequently prevent us from asserting ourselves.

In contrast to respondent behavior, *operant* behavior is an *action* of the organism *on* the environment—a voluntary, purposeful, "emitted" (rather than elicited) response controlled by the central nervous system. Operant behaviors relate particularly to our interactions with other people. The essential characteristic of operant behavior is embodied in the word *do*. Doing encompasses most of our ongoing, daily behavior in commerce with other people, as well as our interactions with our general environment; it includes adaptive as well as unadaptive interpersonal interactions. Operant behavior is controlled by its *consequences;* that is, when the consequences are rewarding, the behavior is strengthened; when they are aversive, the behavior is weakened. We shall discuss these behavioral consequences in greater detail later in the chapter. Two simple examples will clarify the difference between respondent and operant behavior.

Betty—An Example of Respondent Behavior

Betty, a nurse anesthetist, is a fairly well adjusted individual who, like most of us, has a few problem areas. One of her problems is that she becomes anxious when students attend her presentations of clinical cases to other members of the medical staff. Fortunately for Betty, students attend her presentations very rarely, but she never knows in advance when they will be present.

One day, as she walks toward the conference room, Betty hears loud chatter and laughter coming from the room—an indication that a large number of students are there, waiting for her presentation. Immediately, a sickening wave of fear and anxiety sweeps over Betty, and her desperate efforts to remain calm are futile.

This sequence exemplifies Betty's respondent behavior. All that is needed to automatically trigger her emotional discomfort is the eliciting stimulus of the students' laughter and chatter.

Marilyn—An Example of Operant Behavior

Marilyn is a compulsive talker. This fact in itself doesn't really bother her; what disturbs her is that she doesn't know why she talks so much. But an observer of Marilyn's interactions with others would understand her behavior right away. She enjoys the attention she receives from certain individuals, and, although she may not realize it, she tends to seek out and interact more frequently with those who listen to her and give her the attention she needs. Being listened to is rewarding, and, because it follows her talking, it tends to strengthen and maintain that behavior.

Basic Concepts and Terminology
of Operant Conditioning

Most social behavior is operant rather than respondent; that is, it is controlled by its consequences rather than by an eliciting stimulus. Although it may appear voluntary—at times even capricious—operant behavior lends itself to the same precision of prediction and control as respondent behavior. In order to understand how the therapist seeks to predict and control behavior, we must be able to appreciate certain characteristics of the behaviors under consideration. Therefore, a brief review of the basic terminology and principles of operant behavior will be helpful.

First, there are stimuli or events that, when *presented* as a consequence of a response, will increase the occurrence of the response. These stimuli or events are called *positive reinforcers*. Examples of positive reinforcers may include such things as a smile, a pat on the back, or other indicants of favorable social attention. Conversely, there are stimuli or events that, when *removed* as a consequence of a response, will increase the occurrence of that response. These stimuli or events are called *negative reinforcers*. Examples of negative reinforcers include all of those stimuli that the individual may find aversive or painful, such as social rejection or censure. Reinforcement is therefore an operation that strengthens or increases the probability of the recurrence of a response.

Additionally, there are operations that decrease the strength of a response. These operations are *punishment* and *extinction*. Punishment occurs when a *positive* reinforcer is *removed* as a consequence of a response or when a *negative* reinforcer is *presented* as a consequence of a response. Further, if a response occurs that is not followed by reinforcement, that response will extinguish or decrease in strength. In both instances—punishment and extinction—the strength of the response is decreased.

In summary, the strength of an operant response may be increased or decreased through five basic operations:

1. If a positive reinforcer is presented as a consequence of a response, the strength of that response is increased. This operation if called *positive reinforcement*.

2. If a positive reinforcer is withdrawn as a consequence of a response, the strength of that response is decreased. This operation is called *punishment*.

3. If a negative reinforcer is presented as a consequence of a response, the strength of that response is decreased. This operation, too, is called *punishment*.

4. If a negative reinforcer is withdrawn as a consequence of a response, the strength of that response is increased. This operation is called *negative reinforcement*.

5. If a response is not followed by reinforcement, the strength of that response is decreased or eliminated. This operation is called *extinction*.

Reinforcement can be administered continuously (every time the desired response is emitted) or intermittently. *Intermittent reinforcement* is administered only part of the time—that is, not every time the desired response occurs. This type of reinforcement is not as effective for acquisition of the desired behavior as continuous reinforcement, but it leads to a less rapid extinction; in other words, intermittent reinforcement increases resistance to extinction.

One final note should be made before closing this brief "technical" discussion on operant conditioning. When, in the pages that follow, we speak of a *dependent variable*, we are referring to the operant behavior that the therapist is interested in predicting and controlling—in our case, assertive behavior. The events and conditions of which the dependent variable is a function are called *independent variables*—in our case, the events and conditions that affect assertion. When these variables are identified and manipulated, the behavior under consideration can be modified to develop into a more adaptive, assertive behavior. We said "variables" because the control of operant behavior is generally a function of more than one variable (in contrast to the control of respondent behavior, which is a function of just one variable—the eliciting stimulus). In fact, although operant responses are modified primarily through their environmental consequences, the probability of their occurrence may also be dependent on antecedent conditions affecting the organism, on certain drives that exist in the individual, on the habit strength, and on the intensity and other characteristics of the consequences that affect and control that behavior.

Behavior Therapy

All types of psychotherapy seek to help the individual develop more effective coping behavior. As we said earlier, the more traditional types of psychotherapy—particularly psychoanalysis—focus on bringing about changes in the person through conflict resolution and other cognitively oriented techniques; their emphasis is less on modifying the person's present behavior than on helping the individual discover the reasons for such behavior. Behavior therapy, instead, focuses on helping the individual modify unadaptive behavior rather than on exploring inner conflicts and trying to achieve cognitive changes. Thus, behavior modification is carried out by applying general principles of psychology and by employing empirically developed strategies and procedures, with an emphasis on learning principles and techniques. Since assertive training is one form of behavior therapy, it is important that we spend a little time on the development and current status of this major approach to remediation of unadaptive behavior.

The Development and Current Status of Behavior Therapy

One measure of the vigor of a professional discipline or movement is the amount of published material dealing with its orientation, its methods, and its results. As far as behavior therapy is concerned, if the list of suggested readings at the end of this chapter attempted to cover all the publications related to behavior therapy that have appeared in the last few years, including basic research on operant and respondent conditioning, the list would be far longer than the chapter. Even if the list of publications were limited to areas in which behavior control is currently applied, it would still require a very lengthy appendix to this chapter. Therefore, the scope of this book makes it impossible to even attempt a review of the relevant studies on this topic. Suffice it to say that "behavior therapy" is a broad term that encompasses an ever-increasing number of therapeutic techniques aimed at modifying behavior.

We said earlier that behavior therapy, in its various forms, is gaining an increasingly wide acceptance among professionals and lay persons alike. The reason for this increasing popularity may be that the single most important aspect of behavior therapy is its emphasis on an operationally defined, readily observed, and easily measured dependent variable—behavior. By making behavior the focal object of their attention, behavior therapists have provided themselves with a most objective and sensitive indicant of their activities. The specificity of their criterion measure—behavioral change—permits a rather immediate evaluation of both the effects of their efforts and the rate at which they are progressing toward specific therapeutic goals. In other words, in behavior therapy the success of the treatment of problem behavior is measured by the observable change in this behavior—a change that is evaluated in terms of the particular technique being used.

This experimental approach goes a long way toward placing psychotherapy fully within the boundaries of a natural science, subjecting it directly to the empirically derived principles of learning and conditioning. Consequently, while behavior therapy still entails a great deal of "art," the behavior-therapy movement is supported by a rigorously scientific substratum. This art is constantly guided, modified, and improved by the advances that mark basic and applied research in this area. In contrast to those of many traditional and current therapies, the statements constituting behavior therapy's "body of knowledge" are always empirical statements subject to empirical test.

The Rise of Assertive Training

When looking for the antecedents of that form of behavior therapy called assertive training, we must start with Salter's classic book *Conditioned Reflex Therapy* (1949).

Salter's criticisms of psychoanalysis at the beginning of his book are worth quoting. He sees psychoanalysis as employing basically the same procedure whatever the person's problems may be. In addition to this disregard for the uniqueness of each individual's problems, according to Salter there is very little, if any, evidence that analysis is effective. He says:

> It is high time that psychoanalysis, like the elephant of fable, dragged itself off to some distant jungle graveyard and died. Psychoanalysis has outlived its usefulness. Its methods are vague, its treatment is long drawn out, and, more than not, its results are insipid and unimpressive [p. 1].

Salter goes on to urge the development of an excitatory (assertive) personality structure, using principles and procedures derived from Pavlov's classical conditioning, and encourages the development of many specific behaviors that lead toward an assertive style of interaction.

Wolpe, a leading behavior therapist, recommends that individuals deficient in assertive behavior read parts of Salter's book. Wolpe, in his first book, *Psychotherapy by Reciprocal Inhibition* (1958), was the first to actually use the term *assertive training* in print. In regard to its applicability, he stated:

> Assertive training is pre-eminently applicable to the deconditioning of unadaptive anxiety habits of response to people with whom the patient interacts. It makes use of the anxiety-inhibiting emotions that life situations evoke in him. A great many emotions, mostly "pleasant" in character, seem to involve bodily events competitive with anxiety [p. 99].

Wolpe (1958) contended that, with individuals who are anxious and passive in the presence of others, the goal of therapy should be self-assertion. He said:

> The therapist increases the motivation by pointing out the emptiness of the patient's fears, emphasizing how his fearful patterns of behavior have incapacitated him and placed him at the mercy of others, and informing him that, though expression of resentment may be difficult at first, it becomes progressively easier with practice. It usually does not take long for the patient to begin to perform the required behavior, although some need much initial exhortation and repeated promptings [p. 115].

Wolpe sees assertive training as an appropriate treatment procedure in numerous contexts and has often employed it himself in his behavior therapy. He says:

> In almost all of them we find the patient inhibited from the performance of "normal" behavior because of neurotic fear. He is inhibited from saying or doing things that seem reasonable and right to an observer. He may be unable to complain about poor services in a restaurant because he is afraid of hurting the feelings of the waiter; unable to express differences of opinion with his friends because he fears that they will not like him; unable to get up and leave a social situation that has become boring because he fears to seem ungrateful; unable to ask for the repayment of a loan or to administer a reproof to a subordinate because he fears that his "nice guy" image will be impaired; and unable to express affection, admiration, or praise because he finds such expression embarrassing. Besides the things he cannot do because of fear, there may be others that he cannot stop doing. For example, he may compulsively reach for the lunch check again and again to ward off a fear of incurring an obligation [1973, p. 81].*

Lazarus (1973), another prominent behavior therapist, maintains that the main components of assertive (or emotionally expressive) behavior may be divided into four specific and separate response patterns: "(1) the ability to say 'no'; (2) the ability to ask for favors or to make requests; (3) the ability to

*From *The Practice of Behavior Therapy*, by Joseph Wolpe. Copyright 1973 by Pergamon Press, Ltd. Reprinted by permission.

express positive and negative feelings; and (4) the ability to initiate, continue, and terminate general conversations" (p. 697).

In a thorough review of the literature dealing with the development of assertive training, Hersen, Eisler, and Miller (1973) suggest

> that assertive training can be an effective treatment approach for a wide range of disorders including sexual deviation, self-mutilation, impotence, crying spells, and a variety of interpersonal problems. On first examination it is difficult to find a common element underlying these disorders. However, following a careful analysis of the clinical reports, it becomes apparent that these patients are characterized by moderate to severe interpersonal deficits. That is to say, these patients simply do not evidence the requisite social and interpersonal skills to ensure successful functioning. Assertive training then is specifically directed towards teaching patients (regardless of presenting symptomatology or diagnosis) a new mode of responding. When patients become more skilled in routine interpersonal interactions, the probability of obtaining reinforcement from their social milieu is increased. At that point symptomatic behaviors become nonfunctional and are eliminated from their repertoires [p. 518].*

Hersen and his coworkers (1973), in reviewing recent clinical and experimental reports (Eisler, Hersen, & Miller, 1973; Eisler, Miller, & Hersen, 1973; Laws & Serber, 1971; Lazarus, 1971), conclude that not all individuals in need of assertive training behave nonassertively because anxiety inhibits them but, rather, because they have never learned to be assertive; assertion is simply not part of their behavioral repertoire.

Hersen and his coworkers cite Laws and Serber (1971) as arguing that "assertive training with these subjects becomes a process of habituation [the process of learning a new behavior] rather than rehabilitation of old behaviors or facilitation of suppressed behaviors."

In summary, assertive training has developed from an ancillary technique into a major form of behavior therapy. Assertive training employs a variety of procedures that may be applied individually or in a group setting. These procedures are based on the empirical psychology of learning and have evolved from the work of early behavior therapists.

Suggested Readings

Malott, R., Ritterby, K., & Wolf, E. L. *An introduction to behavior modification.* Kalamazoo, Mich.: Behaviordelia, 1973.

Malott, R., & Whaley, D. *Psychology.* New York: Behaviordelia/Harper & Row, 1976.

---

*From "Development of Assertive Responses: Clinical, Measurement, and Research Considerations," by M. Hersen, R. M. Eisler, and P. M. Miller, *Behaviour Research and Therapy*, 1973, *11*(4), 505–521. Copyright 1973. Reprinted by permission of Pergamon Press Ltd.

Rachman, S. *The effects of psychotherapy.* Oxford: Pergamon Press, 1971.

Salter, A. *Conditioned reflex therapy.* New York: Capricorn, 1961. (Originally published, 1949.)

Wenrich, W. W. *A primer of behavior modification.* Monterey, Calif.: Brooks/Cole, 1970.

Whaley, D., & Malott, R. *Elementary principles of behavior.* New York: Appleton-Century-Crofts, 1971.

Wolpe, J. *The practice of behavior therapy.* Oxford: Pergamon Press, 1973.

Chapter Three / Adaptive versus unadaptive behavior

Topic Overview

I. Adaptive and unadaptive behavior
   1. Cultural relativity and idiosyncratic views play a relevant role in determining whether a behavior is adaptive or unadaptive.
   2. Adaptive behavior represents a balance between the individual's needs and society's demands; it is functional and effective in a given context, does not result in discomfort to the individual or to others, and is in harmony with society's structure.
   3. Unadaptive behavior goes counter to the needs and goals of the individual and to those of society; it is dysfunctional and ineffective in a given context, causes discomfort and even distress to the individual and often to others, and may be very disruptive to society's structure.

II. Assertiveness as adaptive behavior and nonassertiveness as unadaptive behavior
   1. Assertiveness is standing up for one's own rights, without infringing upon the rights of others. It is adaptive behavior because it is functional in a given context, is self-enhancing, generates positive feelings toward oneself and others, and leads to smooth interpersonal relationships.
   2. Nonassertiveness is not standing up for one's rights when they are infringed upon. It is unadaptive behavior because it is dysfunctional in a given context, is self-denying, generates anxiety and negative feelings toward oneself and others, and leads to strained interpersonal relationships.

III. Nonassertiveness
1. *Like most behaviors, nonassertiveness can be explained in terms of learning. People can be conditioned to become nonassertive.*
2. *Salter discussed nonassertiveness in terms of excessive inhibitions.*
3. *Nonassertiveness can be situational (limited to specific contexts) or general (extending to all or most of one's daily interactions).*

IV. Aggressiveness
1. *Aggressiveness is the tendency to display offensive, hostile behaviors against others, without regard for their rights.*
2. *Aggressiveness should not be confused with assertiveness. While the latter is a positive and adaptive behavior, the former is a negative, unadaptive behavior.*
3. *Aggressiveness is unadaptive behavior because it is dysfunctional in a given context, generates negative feelings—such as guilt, remorse, fear of consequences, and alienation—causes constant confrontation with others, and leads to shallow emotional ties.*
4. *Aggressiveness can be situational or general.*

— Adaptive behavior is often defined as the capacity to live in harmony with the environment—adjusting to change without major difficulty and achieving, at least to some degree, most of one's goals. But what constitutes adaptive behavior depends to a large extent on who is making the evaluation. In the same society, a behavior may be viewed as adaptive or unadaptive by some but not by others, and the view often undergoes significant changes in the course of time. Homosexuality, for example, is considered as a form of unadaptive behavior by many segments of our society today; it is not, however, seen as such by other, albeit smaller, segments of the society, and in our own culture the view of homosexuality has undergone profound changes in the course of history. "Dropping out" and seeking personal satisfaction as opposed to material goals are viewed by some as an efficient and satisfactory way of coping with life; by others—possibly the vast majority, we may add—as very unadaptive behavior. Similarly, seeking success and monetary rewards is considered adaptive or unadaptive behavior depending on the segment of the society that does the judging.

Cultural relativity, therefore, plays an important role in determining what is adaptive behavior, and so does the individual's own bias—what we may call the "idiosyncratic" view of behavior. The hermit who lives on top of a mountain in complete isolation, without any of the amenities of life, might well view his own behavior as highly adaptive, since it permits him to achieve the life-style that he has set for himself and that he considers productive and satisfying. The majority of us, however, would consider the hermit's behavior as highly unadaptive, since it runs contrary to the basic premises on which our view of life is based and is therefore incompatible with our society's goals and with the role we assign to the individual in our society.

Do cultural relativity and the idiosyncratic approach thus make a definition of adaptive behavior impossible? We don't think so. All human beings have needs, urges, and impulses that strive for expression but that are controlled, to a greater or lesser degree, by societal mores, rules, and regulations. Therefore, another—and, in our view, more meaningful—way of looking at adaptive behavior is in terms of maintaining a balance between one's needs and society's demands. From this viewpoint, adaptive behavior is a behavior that is functional and effective in a given context, that does not result in abrasion or discomfort to the individual or to others, and that does not disrupt society's structure. Unadaptive behavior is just the opposite of all the descriptors we have used for adaptive behavior. It is dysfunctional and ineffective in a given context, results in discomfort and even distress to the individual and often to others, and may be so disruptive to society's structure as to invite the intervention of social agents. Unadaptive behavior goes counter to the needs and goals of the individual and to those of society. It is characterized by the frustration and discomfort that the nonattainment of one's goals produces and results in confusion, anxiety, dissatisfaction, and low efficiency. In sum, unadaptive behavior is responsible for a large share of the problems people experience with themselves and in their interactions with others.

This chapter discusses assertiveness as an example of adaptive behavior and nonassertiveness and aggressiveness as examples of unadaptive behavior.

Assertiveness as Adaptive Behavior and Nonassertiveness as Unadaptive Behavior

All of us, as human beings and as citizens of a free country, have certain inalienable rights—from those guaranteed by law, such as freedom of speech and the right to a due process of law, to the more subtle rights to stand up for our views or to act in our own best interest. In our everyday life, we are often confronted with situations that violate, or at least threaten, some of our rights. An assertive person knows how to stand up for and does stand up for his or her rights.

Suppose, for example, that you are deeply involved in a discussion of an important issue with someone whose opinion you value. George, an acquaintance of yours, walks up to you and interrupts your conversation to interject his uninvited views, thus preventing you from carrying on your original discussion. What, under the circumstances, would an assertive response be? An assertive response would be to tell George, politely but firmly, that right now you are engaged in an important conversation with someone else—a conversation you want to pursue—and that you would appreciate it if he chose another occasion to talk with you or waited until you have finished talking with the other person. Neither letting the situation go unchallenged nor telling your acquaintance off would be an example of assertive behavior. In the former instance, you would fail to stand up for your right to express your true feelings and to act in your best interest; in the latter, you would be likely to cause discomfort to another person. In sum, assertiveness is standing up for one's own rights, without infringing upon the rights of others.

Nonassertiveness, instead, is the incapacity to act as one would like to, the holding back and refraining from expressing one's own feelings and thoughts because of fear, inhibition, or modesty or simply as a result of being taught not to be assertive or never having learned to assert oneself. In sum, nonassertiveness is not standing up for one's own rights when they are infringed upon.

Suppose, for example, that you brought your car to a garage for a tune-up. You pick up the car, pay for the service, and leave. As you drive home, you realize that the car is not running as smoothly as should be expected after a tune-up. What would a nonassertive response be? A nonassertive response would be for you to keep the car in poor running condition, say nothing to the garage manager or mechanic, and swear to yourself that you'll never use that garage again. You do nothing about the situation and you deny yourself the right to expect a service that is worth the money you paid for it. As an assertive person, you would go back to the garage and inform the manager or the mechanic that you are not satisfied with the job and that you feel that either your car should be tuned-up correctly or your money should be refunded.

The title of this section equates assertiveness with adaptive behavior and nonassertiveness with unadaptive behavior. Although the reason for this may be self-evident, let's spend a few moments on this very important point in our discussion. We said earlier that adaptive behavior permits the person to maintain a balance between his or her own needs and society's demands, that it is functional in a given context, and that it does not result in abrasion or discomfort to the person and to others. The assertive behavior we outlined in our first example meets all of these requirements. Your need to act in your best interest and to express your true feelings is satisfied, and so is society's demand that one be polite to others. It is functional because it permits you to carry on your conversation with your friend and does not cause discomfort to you or to your importunate acquaintance. As a result, you are likely to feel satisfied with yourself because you handled the situation well and because you can pursue your discussion, and George (if he is a reasonable person), recognizing the validity of your stand and appreciating your politeness, does not feel unduly embarrassed or hurt. If instead you had behaved nonassertively, not only would you have felt frustrated and inadequate, but most likely you would have been quite angry with George, who, in turn, would have sensed your resentment without understanding why you were angry with him.

Figure 1 shows the pattern illustrated in our examples by providing a brief description of the feelings and outcomes characteristic of adaptive and unadaptive behavior, specifically of assertiveness and nonassertiveness. The figure also includes a description of the outcomes of aggressiveness, another kind of unadaptive behavior, which we'll discuss in detail later in the chapter.

Situation	Behavioral response	Outcomes
Typical interpersonal situation calling for assertive response	*Nonassertiveness (unadaptive)*	Self-denial, withdrawal, feelings of inadequacy and helplessness, anxiety, lack of spontaneity, pent-up negative emotions, strained interpersonal relationships
	Assertiveness (adaptive)	Feelings of adequacy and mastery of environment, positive feelings toward oneself and others, spontaneity, smooth interpersonal relationships
	Aggressiveness (unadaptive)	Guilt, remorse, fear of consequences, anxiety, hypertension, withdrawal, alienation, lack of meaningful relationships

Figure 1   Characteristics of adaptive and unadaptive behavior

Nonassertiveness

In the pages that follow, we deal at length with nonassertive behavior. This discussion, largely based on the views expressed by writers in the field of assertive and nonassertive behavior, is intended to define and illustrate as clearly as possible the behavioral traits of the nonassertive individual and their causes. We believe that, without an adequate understanding of what constitutes nonassertiveness, any attempt at understanding the alternative—assertiveness—and at learning its values and techniques would be futile. One very important point we wish to make before beginning our discussion is that, in writing about nonassertive behavior, we are pointing at the unadaptive behavior of those who are *unable* to assert themselves and therefore have no choice but to be nonassertive. Not to assert oneself can, under certain circumstances, be a form of adaptive behavior. People who *elect* not to assert themselves but who have the ability to be assertive if they so desire are not engaging in unadaptive behavior.

Nonassertive behavior, like most behaviors, can be explained to a large extent in terms of learning. Nonassertive people either have not learned (which means that they have not been taught) to assert themselves or have been conditioned not to assert themselves by being taught that assertive behavior is undesirable. Efforts at self-assertion thus become sources of fear, anxiety, and guilt. Women and members of certain minorities in this country have been prime targets of this kind of conditioning; their struggles for self-assertion are indicative of the power of the conditioning and of the difficulty of overcoming—as individuals, as groups, and as members of the society—its destructive effects.

In the previous chapter, we outlined some of the principles of conditioning, and we said that reinforcers strengthen a behavior and punishment tends to eliminate it. Conditioning people to be nonassertive follows these same general rules. In our culture, for example, women have been conditioned to see themselves as nonassertive, and both reinforcers and punishment have been consistently used by society to make this conditioning work. Early-age indoctrination about well-defined sex roles, praise for behavior that adheres to these roles and disapproval of behavior that defies them, and tremendous resistance to women's attempts at breaking the mold of nonassertiveness are very familiar examples of this conditioning technique. If the technique works, the result is a nonassertive individual—self-denying, inhibited, filled with anxiety and guilt every time she attempts to be assertive.

The credit for writing the first treatment of nonassertiveness and assertiveness (which he called "inhibition" and "excitation," respectively) goes to Salter. He dealt with this topic in *Conditioned Reflex Therapy*, published in 1949—a book that is a must for anyone interested in the development of assertive behavior and that has influenced many later works, including this one. Although we do not agree with many of Salter's views and feel that more research is necessary to support the Pavlovian position expressed in his book, he must be recognized, as we said earlier, as the pioneer in the area of assertive training. According to Salter,

> Actually, the first person who ever wrote about assertion was a woman patient of mine. On January 3, 1942, in her first entry in the assertion diary she kept for me, she wrote, "Why wait until tomorrow to start asserting yourself. Here's a perfect set-up for you." Consequently, the historical priorities of this form of therapy and of the use of the word "assertion" to describe it may be considered as settled. This diary covers 9½ single-spaced pages, and its "modernity" is extraordinary [Salter, personal communication, 1975].

Salter says that people with excessive inhibitions (who are nonassertive, to use the current terminology) lead a sad and unhappy life. They are watchers rather than doers, and life passes them by without their knowing its richness. They generally experience a sense of emptiness, a lack of fulfillment, and a feeling of dissatisfaction. Also, overly inhibited people (Salter calls them "inhibitory") tend to suffer from psychosomatic and psychophysiological disorders, such as chronic headaches, constipation, and insomnia. The inhibitory individual, says Salter, often rationalizes his behavior as an expression of his desire for acceptance by others. And yet, no matter how strongly he seeks acceptance, the inhibitory seldom achieves it; the very goal he fervently seeks eludes him. His fear of expressing his true feelings—his inhibitions—makes him unpleasant to associate with, and the discomfort he feels when he tries to express his feelings makes him avoid meaningful relationships. It is this difficulty in expressing his feelings—especially when he is upset, angry, or hurt—that makes him "uptight." Salter notes "The inhibitory are like flypaper. A harsh glance, an overlooked letter, an imagined slight, stick in their minds, and the more they try to shake them off ('Why should I let such little things bother me?') the more firmly stuck they become. They do not vomit forth nauseating emotional food. They try to digest it, and it makes them sick" (pp. 48–49).

The nonassertive individual *cannot* respond freely in the give and take of everyday interactions. He is like a boxer who has to pause and think before he throws a punch at his opponent and, as a result, is clobbered. In interpersonal situations, he is generally outmatched and outclassed, much like a bush-league amateur trying to make it in the big league. The nonassertive person lacks the basic zest and spark of life—spontaneity. His responses are either entirely inhibited or "too little too late." The frustration and emotional discomfort that result from this lack of spontaneity become even more intense because they are not expressed, and the headaches, neckaches, and other uncomfortable physical reactions continue.

In describing inhibitory individuals, Salter points to the fact that they behave in the same way no matter how important or how trivial a situation may be:

> They're the last to enter, and the last to leave an elevator. They are always apologetic. They are exploited, toiling at tedious tasks. They poison themselves with resentment for years before asking for a wage increase. They are pathetic with waiters, barbers, and salesmen, and they have as much difficulty with their mother-in-law. They are the women who go into a dress shop and buy in order to get out. As one of them put it, "I've been refusing second portions all my life." They constantly fear that they are inconveniencing people and attracting attention. They fear that they're taking up too much air [p. 49].

Situational and General Nonassertiveness

Nonassertiveness may be situational or general. This very important point was well clarified by two other writers on assertive behavior, Robert Alberti and Michael Emmons (1970), in their book entitled *Your Perfect Right*. Situational nonassertiveness refers to the behavior of individuals who are generally adequately adjusted but who have difficulty in asserting themselves in specific contexts; they can assert themselves in some situations but not in others. Remember, *most of us are situationally nonassertive to some degree*. An example of situational nonassertiveness is the successful businessman who can assert himself easily at work but finds it impossible to assert himself at home. Situationally nonassertive individuals are usually quite aware of the specific nature of their difficulty yet are at a loss as to how to change their behavior. Such people are generally good candidates for assertive training.

General nonassertiveness refers to the behavior of individuals who are nonassertive in all or most of their daily interactions. They usually have a philosophy of life that fosters nonassertiveness; their values and attitudes seem to be patterned after the slogan "The meek shall inherit the earth." Thus, they have virtually eliminated all assertive responses from their behavioral repertoire. Unlike situationally nonassertive individuals, they do not experience the anger, resentment, and other feelings of frustration that certain situations would normally call for. When anger is experienced, it is immediately inhibited and replaced by shame, guilt, and anxiety. Salter (1949) has lucidly described these individuals as follows: "The inhibitory have developed the brake habit. They have collided with too many automobiles on the highway of life, and have learned to drive with the brake on" (p. 54).

To become assertive, generally nonassertive individuals require greater efforts than situationally nonassertive persons. Their basic values and life styles need to be revamped if assertive techniques are to be developed. Situationally nonassertive persons, instead, need only to work in developing assertive behavior in certain particular situations.

The following two examples should clarify the differences between situational and general nonassertiveness.

Paul—An Example of Situational Nonassertiveness

Paul is a moderately successful insurance broker who labored long and hard to arrive at his present station in life. He makes an adequate income, is happily married and has two children, and thinks of himself as being generally successful in achieving the goals he sets for himself. Looking at his career, at his income, and at his family, one would not hesitate to say that, at 35, Paul has indeed "arrived." Yet, Paul is a very unhappy individual and suffers from periods of moderate to severe depression. During these times he often wonders what went wrong in his life.

Let's look more closely at Paul. In spite of his accomplishments, which would make most people feel quite satisfied, Paul has a problem that often makes these accomplishments seem worthless. This problem lies in the area of interpersonal interaction, specifically in his inability to respond assertively in certain situations; he finds it extremely difficult to assert himself (to express his views effectively and to stand up for them) in the presence of several people. Paul has always been a low-keyed, easy-going individual, whose quiet personality and conscientiousness have been assets to both his college and his business careers. His reputation as a loyal, reliable, and competent worker has been largely responsible for his fairly rapid rise to his present position. Yet, all along Paul has had difficulty in asserting himself in the presence of several persons. Until recently, he has generally been able to avoid such situations and thus minimize his discomfort. Now he can't do it anymore, because his job responsibilities require his attending meetings where he must present and defend his views on various issues. In these situations, his fear of asserting himself prevents him from effectively stating and maintaining his views and from challenging others, even when he thinks that they are wrong. Insecurity and anxiety govern his conduct at these meetings, and the resulting frustration intensifies his inhibitions. In turn, this failure to appropriately handle the situation triggers off his periodic depressive reactions that make him feel helpless, hurt, and worthless.

Paul is aware of his problem and, although he realizes that, in various forms and to a greater or lesser extent, it is a fairly common one, wants to do something about it because it involves his job and thus significantly affects an important area of his life, and, even more disturbing, it undermines his own self-concept.

Isabel—An Example of General Nonassertiveness

Isabel, a twenty-three-year-old college student, is a very unhappy person. There are several reasons for her unhappiness, most of them dealing with her belief that people "use her." Isabel thinks of herself as being kind, considerate, and helpful; she never hesitates to do favors when asked, no matter how unreasonable the request may be, and she finds it virtually impossible to say no. Having been raised in a family in which nonassertiveness was stressed and the children were taught that it is better to be a good listener than a talker, Isabel is a quiet, overly modest person, always careful not to interrupt others, even if this means hardly ever expressing her own views. Because of her concern about "offending" someone, she is chronically tense and anxious lest she should say or not say the "right" thing. Friends and fellow students frequently borrow books and other material from her and seldom, if ever, return them. The fact that she cannot assert herself in any situation makes her life pretty miserable. And yet, Isabel thinks that the problem lies with others who use her, not with herself. She does not realize that she is a generally nonassertive person and, as such, in need of help.

Aggressiveness

Aggressiveness (the tendency to display aggression) is one of those terms used loosely by professionals and lay persons alike. One of the most common misuses of the word is as a synonym for assertiveness. Even though the two behaviors share certain characteristics, assertiveness and aggressiveness should not be confused. Their differences can be subsumed under the labels of positive/adaptive and negative/unadaptive; assertiveness is a positive and adaptive behavior; aggressiveness, a negative and unadaptive behavior.

Aggression has been defined in different ways by different theorists, depending on their orientation. For the purpose of our discussion, we define aggression as an offensive, hostile action against another, in disregard of his or her rights. Aggression is characterized by the desire to pursue one's goals at whatever cost to the rights and welfare of others.

Albert Ellis, a prominent psychologist, in addressing the 1973 Annual Convention of the American Psychological Association, stated that psychologists (and related specialists) need to better define their use of the word *aggression* and to distinguish its "healthy" and "unhealthy" aspects. Ellis described various forms of aggression, such as

1. *Annoyance.* Largely a negative feeling but often a realistically appropriate response to a threatening situation; since it usually helps the individual improve or change his situation, it is a healthy response.
2. *Argumentativeness.* Occasionally healthy in that the individual stands up for his views; when carried to extremes, it becomes overassertiveness and thus overlaps domineeringness and is unhealthy.
3. *Assertiveness.* Highly desirable behavior—perhaps the healthiest form of aggression.

Many psychologists, according to Ellis, use the word *aggression* when they should use, more appropriately, the word *assertion*. The key to correctly conceptualizing these two terms is to think of assertiveness as a goal-getting adaptive behavior and of aggressiveness as a frustrating and self-defeating unadaptive behavior. Aggression, Ellis (1973) noted, may range from "mild argumentativeness to severe oppositionalism; from healthy assertion to unhealthy domineering; from positive to negative defensiveness; from moderate irritation to extreme hostility; from moderate combativeness to intense violence; from verbal arrogance or insult to murderous fury." He continued: "Almost everything good that has been and can be said about aggression can fairly easily be subsumed under the label of assertion."

Examples of the unfortunate confusion between assertive and aggressive behavior are common; in both popular and professional literature reference is often made to "dynamic, forceful, and aggressive" behavior. Our society highly values the self-reliant, forceful person who can overcome obstacles and achieve goals. Most if not all of the benefits that accrue from this "dynamic, forceful, and aggressive" behavior actually result from assertive and not from aggressive behavior.

The negative concomitants of aggressive behavior are almost too obvious to enumerate. The caustically insulting individual may "put down" his opponents but soon discovers that they can strike back at him in other ways. The violent person may have the satisfaction of releasing his hostility by punching someone in the mouth but may find himself in jail for criminal assault. In short, the aggressive individual obtains his immediate goal at the expense of others and in the long run at his own expense. This is not to say that there may not be occasions when aggressive behavior is justified or even necessary, but in our daily interactions an aggressive life-style is generally unproductive. For most aggressive individuals, constant confrontation, alienation, subtle or direct ostracism, and shallow emotional ties are the sad results of their unadaptive behavior.

Situational and General Aggressiveness

Just as nonassertiveness may be general or situational, aggressiveness too may be limited to specific situations or extend to a generalized behavioral response pattern. In situational aggression, people behave aggressively only in specific instances—for example, in dealing with subordinates. They may then fly into a rage at the slightest opportunity and abuse the subordinate. It is important to keep in mind that, since aggression is based on selfish concerns and on a disregard for the rights of others, these individuals do not attempt to explain their behavior, which may be quite deliberate or impulsive. Aggressive people may realize that their behavior is inappropriate but are generally at a loss as to how to change it.

In general aggressiveness, the individual's very values and attitudes support the maintenance of aggressive behavior. Aggressiveness is a pervasive personality characteristic, and this type of person responds to virtually all situations in an aggressive manner. Typically, he has been raised in an environment in which the significant others (those he identified with and whose behavior he tried to copy) related with other people in an aggressive manner. Simply stated, generally aggressive individuals have learned to relate aggressively with others; they take pride in their aggressiveness, even though it causes them discomfort from strained social relationships. Their value structure places a premium on aggressiveness and regards assertiveness as a manifestation of lack of courage, even as a form of cowardice. Like the generally nonassertive person, the generally aggressive individual requires much effort to change to a more adaptive style of interaction. The techniques used in assertive training (which are discussed in Part Two of this book) are helpful in bringing this change about.

John—An Example of Situational Aggressiveness

John is a fairly pleasant, congenial individual who interacts quite well with people. One exception to John's adaptive behavior is his attitude toward subordinates and people in the service trades, such as bank clerks, waiters, and sales persons. From them John expects prompt and impeccable service; any delay, fumbling, or disagreement elicits an immediate aggressive response on his part, so immediate as to be almost automatic. His attacks are very personal in nature and are designed to hurt. John does not know the reasons for his behavior. Since in most other situations he is not aggressive, people who know him are very surprised when they witness these episodes of aggressiveness.

Nancy—An Example of General Aggressiveness

Nancy is bright, well educated, attractive—and very lonely. She prides herself in the fact that, as far as she can remember, no one has been able to "get to her." She has a sharp, biting tongue, which she uses mercilessly against anybody who dares to stand up to her. She is intelligent enough to exercise some control over her aggressiveness, particularly with people who may be able to make her suffer the consequences of her behavior—such as a teacher or an employer. But, aside from these special cases, she dispenses her acid and humiliating comments to anyone who, for one reason or another, incurs her wrath. As a result, people fear and dislike Nancy intensely, and she is a very lonely and unhappy woman, in spite of the fact that, beneath all that hostility and aggressiveness, there is a warm and generous person. There are times when she would like to be accepted by others, but the wary distance others keep from her serves only to intensify her hostility.

Nancy knows that something is wrong with her, and yet she cannot understand why her behavior is so self-defeating. She grew up in an environment where aggressiveness was considered a desirable quality and the respect for the rights of others as a sign of weakness. In her eyes, her behavior is appropriate, and she cannot understand why people avoid her.

In the preceding pages, we have discussed at length adaptive and unadaptive behavior and described nonassertiveness, aggressiveness, and assertiveness. The following case examples should help clarify even further the differences among these three kinds of behavior.

Example One

Barry, an easy-going file clerk, works in an office with 12 other file clerks. Each clerk has responsibility for filing a prescribed number of records every day. Barry, because he is either more conscientious or more efficient than his fellow workers, is able to file a third more records each day than the others. Two of the other clerks, Benjamin and Karl, have become accustomed to bringing some of their work to Barry, stating that they "just can't get to it." This irritates Barry because it adds to his work and because he doesn't like Benjamin's and Karl's lazy attitude, particularly in view of the fact that one day he overheard them joking about how clever they were in getting Barry to do their work. Resentment has been building in Barry for some time and now has reached the point where it is seriously bothering him.

Nonassertive Response

Barry continues to work at his usual pace, doing the extra work in addition to his own, and not saying anything to either Benjamin or Karl. He tries to rationalize his behavior by saying to himself that he doesn't really mind the extra work and that, in any case, he gets paid to work eight hours a day and that's what he is doing. But this and other rationalizations don't work that well. As time goes by, Barry looks more and more upset. Benjamin and Karl, suspecting the truth, one day ask him if their adding to his work bothers him. Barry can't bring himself to express his true feelings and laughs off the question. Needless to say, Benjamin and Karl keep "sharing their work" with Barry.

Aggressive Response

Barry ponders his situation over. The more he thinks about it, the more upset he becomes with the fact that he is doing more than his fair share; resentment builds up and turns into hostility toward Benjamin and Karl. But he doesn't say anything to them to indicate his displeasure and keeps working and sulking. Finally, on a day that Barry feels particularly angry, Benjamin brings over some records and asks Barry to file them for him. Without any warning, Barry explodes into a tirade against Benjamin. "You no-good lazy son of a bitch," Barry screams, "I've done your damn work too long, and I'm tired of it." Benjamin's feeble attempt to find out why Barry is so mad seems to only infuriate him more. All Barry wants is to get his hostility off his chest; he continues to rail Benjamin and then starts with Karl until, completely exhausted and still shaking, he suddenly stops. Benjamin and, by this time, Karl look at him in stunned disbelief. "Why haven't you said something about this earlier?" they ask when they can finally put a word in. Barry stands there feeling awkward and not knowing what to say.

Assertive Response

After working under the above circumstances for a brief period of time and realizing that Benjamin and Karl will not change, Barry decides to put an end to a situation that he finds intolerable. He chooses a time when he, Benjamin, and Karl are alone and, without evasions, he begins "It's not that I don't enjoy working with you, for I do; but I must tell you that I'm irritated with having to do part of your work along with my own." He goes on to say that he feels it is only fair that they do their share of work, just as he does his. Benjamin and Karl, appreciating Barry's forthright manner, say that they see his point and understand how he feels. "Good," replies Barry, "I'm sure that you also agree with me when I say that from now on I will not be doing any of your work." Benjamin and Karl reply that they do and that in the future they will do their work and leave Barry alone to do his. They part, each feeling comfortable with the way the situation was handled.

Example Two

Betty has worked hard all her life. After her parents died, she raised a younger sister, Katherine; when Katherine got married, Betty started and slowly built up a modestly successful catering business and an equally modest savings. Betty believed in the value and rewards of hard work; she looked forward to some leisure and, most of all, to traveling abroad. But over the years her savings have been reduced by her sister, who has borrowed money for various "emergencies"—a new color TV or an addition to her home—and has never returned it. Every year Betty drives her old car and watches her vacation recede farther into the future; every year Katherine's family takes a vacation and buys a new car.

Nonassertive Response

Betty continues to work and save and never mentions the borrowed money to Katherine. She keeps telling herself that Katherine will repay all the loans, despite the fact that Katherine not only fails to return, or even talk about returning, the money but recently asked Betty for another loan "for just a few days." Betty, despite her doubts that she'll ever see the money again, loans the money and immediately regrets it. Her savings are once again almost gone, yet she does not have the courage to ask Katherine to repay the money or part of it. At times, she suspects that she will be making further loans for the rest of her life.

Aggressive Response

As Betty continues to read travel folders describing tours that she cannot afford, her resentment at Katherine grows to the point that she can hardly control it. She makes no attempt to talk to Katherine about the money, although she has had several opportunities. Betty rationalizes her inaction by saying that Katherine shouldn't be told to return borrowed money. Finally her resentment erupts one day as she runs into Katherine at the supermarket, and she launches a verbal attack on her sister, right in the middle of a discussion about the high cost of pork. She says that Katherine spends far too much money on expensive meats and other things; as a matter of fact, she spends far too much money, period; that she is a terrible homemaker, and that her children are "spoiled rotten." She mentions only in passing her anger at Katherine for not repaying her loans. Katherine is flabbergasted and can't figure out why her sister has launched such an "unprovoked" attack on her.

Assertive Response

Betty decides to talk with her sister about the money. She waits when they are alone at Betty's house, and she begins by telling Katherine how much she values their relationship. She explains that it is partly because she values her sister and their relationship that she cannot tolerate any longer a situation that makes her feel very angry toward her. She then talks specifically about the loaned money and about the fact that the loans were made with the clear understanding that the money would be returned within a reasonable length of time. Betty tells Katherine that she has worked hard all her life for that money and that now she wants to enjoy some of the fruits of her labor. She asks Katherine when she thinks she will repay her debts; when Katherine replies quite vaguely, Betty asks for a specific time, and they finally agree that Katherine will repay her debt in three installments, setting specific amounts and dates.

The following 12 situations call for assertive behavior. After reading about each situation, write on a sheet of paper the assertive response you think appropriate for the situation.

1. You are in a crowded restaurant, patiently waiting to be served, when you notice that several people who came after you have already been served. Time passes, and you still have not been served, in spite of the fact that you ordered a simple dish that didn't require any lengthy preparation. You have grown very impatient and annoyed.
2. You are a very good tennis player. Your friend Susan, with whom you often play, keeps saying that she would love to play with someone who is a match for her skills, thus implying that you are not. Your opinion is that Susan is a third-rate player.
3. You are telling a joke to a group of friends, when Scott interrupts you and delivers the punch line before you are half-way through telling the joke.
4. You have asked the office secretary to type an important report for you, and a colleague of yours tells the secretary to stop typing your report and do some work for him right away.
5. You are waiting in line at a theater, when the couple in front of you invites three friends to join them in the line ahead of you. You know that the theater is almost full and that only a few tickets are still available.
6. You have asked your mother-in-law not to give little Elliott a piece of chocolate cake, because it will spoil his dinner. She says that she made the cake especially for Elliott and gives him a piece.

7. You go to an appliance store the day of their annual clearance sale. You are one of the first people there. When you tell the salesman that you are interested in one of their six color-television sets advertised at a reduced price, he tells you that all of them have already been sold but that he will be glad to show you some other, more expensive sets.
8. Your boss is very disorganized and ends up doing most of his work in the late afternoon. As a consequence, he asks you all the time to stay after hours to finish something "urgent." You like your job and don't want to quit; on the other hand, you cannot tolerate the situation any longer.
9. Cathy, a friend of yours, has a habit of dropping in unexpectedly at all times of the day. You like Cathy but dislike very much her barging in on you.
10. You are looking forward to playing golf with some friends on Saturday. When you come home Friday night, your wife, who knew about your plans, tells you that she has accepted an invitation to lunch on Saturday for both of you.
11. Both you and your husband work full time and share in the house chores. He is supposed to take care of breakfast. For several days now, you have had to fix breakfast yourself or go to work on an empty stomach because he "overslept."
12. A teacher gives you a C on a test, and you are sure that you deserve a much better grade.

Did you write down how you would apply assertive behavior in all of the above situations? When you have finished reading this book, come back to these 12 situations, respond assertively to each of them again, and then compare the two sets of answers. Have they changed? If so, what do these changes indicate?

Part Two / Practical applications

Chapter Four / Preparing for assertive training

Topic Overview

I. Behavioral analysis is a procedure aimed at identifying unadaptive behavior and represents the first step in assertive training. Techniques one can employ to analyze one's own behavior are:
  1. The Assertive Behavior Checklist, which permits one to readily identify verbal and nonverbal unadaptive behavior.
  2. The Assertive Behavior Record Form, which is used to record one's behavior over a given period of time to identify instances of unadaptive responses and to indicate the assertive response one would have liked to have made in each particular situation.
  3. Rathus Assertiveness Schedule, which is a standardized instrument useful for determining how assertive one is.

II. Being able to correctly identify one's behavior as assertive, nonassertive, or aggressive is another essential step in assertive training. The techniques one can employ to this effect are:
  1. Use of an "outside observer"—that is, asking oneself how an outside observer would view the behavior in question.
  2. Feedback from the therapist (if one is seeing a professional).
  3. Feedback from the person one is interacting with.
  4. Feedback from "significant others" (spouse, friends, and relatives).

III. Reality testing is a further means of correctly identifying one's behavior; it refers to the validation of one's perceptions against some external source.

IV. Cognitive restructuring involves the replacement of beliefs and attitudes that maintain unadaptive behavior with others that are more conducive to the desired behavioral change. Cognitive restructuring, although not *sufficient for the development of assertive behavior, sets the stage for such development by permitting the individual to be more receptive to behavioral change.*

Assertive training involves not only a change of behavior but also a change of beliefs and attitudes. The individual in need of assertive training must believe in the value of assertiveness or, at the very least, not hold a strong opposing belief. When his or her attitude is appropriate, behavioral change is easier. This change is a gradual, incremental procedure in which unadaptive behavior gives way to adaptive behavior and, upon completion of training, situations that formerly elicited nonassertive or aggressive responses are met instead with assertive responses. This pattern of adaptive behavior, with its concomitant positive feelings of control and mastery, becomes a well-established part of the individual's repertoire.

Behavioral Analysis

Behavioral analysis is a procedure crucial to all behavior therapy. As its name suggests, behavioral analysis is the analysis of behavior, focusing on unadaptive components and determining the variables most likely to effect a change resulting in more adaptive behavioral patterns. A thorough behavioral analysis precedes all behavior therapy. What specific, objectively defined problem does the individual have? What variables are maintaining the unadaptive behavior? What adaptive behavior should be looked upon as the goal of therapy? What are the most effective techniques to be employed in bringing about the modification? These questions and many others are posed and answered in the behavioral analysis of an individual.

Assertive Behavior Checklist

In assertive training, behavioral analysis focuses on the verbal and nonverbal behavior of the individual. The Assertive Behavior Checklist provided below is a form designed to permit a quick assessment of one's own behavior. After reading this far, you should know enough about assertive, nonassertive, and aggressive behavior to be able to use the checklist to determine which of your behaviors are not as assertive as you feel they should be. Each behavior is identified with the numbers 1 through 3. Number 1 refers to an adaptive (assertive) behavior; number 2 refers to an unadaptive (nonassertive or aggressive) behavior; and number 3 indicates that you are not sure. The form can help you identify some of your behaviors that may need modification. Simply read the list and put a check in the space by the number that you think indicates whether your behavior is adaptive or unadaptive; if you are not sure, put a check by number 3.

　　　After completing the Assertive Behavior Checklist, study it to identify the unadaptive behaviors you believe you are engaging in. Write these behaviors in the space provided at the bottom of the checklist; they represent your target behavior, and your efforts will be directed toward modifying them. For the professionals reading this book, the checklist can provide an expedient method of "zeroing in" on unadaptive behavior. Each of the behaviors listed below will be described in detail in Chapter Five, which is devoted to assertive verbal and nonverbal behavior.

ASSERTIVE BEHAVIOR CHECKLIST

I. *Verbal Behavior*

A. Loudness of Voice

Adaptive	Unadaptive	Not Sure
1_____	2_____	3_____

B. Fluency of Speech

Adaptive	Unadaptive	Not Sure
1_____	2_____	3_____

C. Use of Personal Pronoun "I"

Adaptive	Unadaptive	Not Sure
1_____	2_____	3_____

D. Expressing Positive Feelings

　　a. Paying Compliments

Adaptive	Unadaptive	Not Sure
1_____	2_____	3_____

　　b. Expressing Affection

Adaptive	Unadaptive	Not Sure
1_____	2_____	3_____

　　c. Expressing Empathy

Adaptive	Unadaptive	Not Sure
1_____	2_____	3_____

　　d. Giving and Encouraging Greeting Expressions

Adaptive	Unadaptive	Not Sure
1_____	2_____	3_____

E. Initiating Conversation

Adaptive	Unadaptive	Not Sure
1_____	2_____	3_____

F. Maintaining Control of Conversation

Adaptive	Unadaptive	Not Sure
1_____	2_____	3_____

G. Talking Extemporaneously

Adaptive	Unadaptive	Not Sure
1_____	2_____	3_____

H. Expressing Emotions

Adaptive	Unadaptive	Not Sure
1_____	2_____	3_____

I. Talking about Oneself
    Adaptive   Unadaptive   Not Sure
    1_____   2_____   3_____
J. Feeling Talk and Emotional Honesty
    Adaptive   Unadaptive   Not Sure
    1_____   2_____   3_____
K. Agreeing with Compliments
    Adaptive   Unadaptive   Not Sure
    1_____   2_____   3_____
L. Disagreeing Passively
    Adaptive   Unadaptive   Not Sure
    1_____   2_____   3_____
M. Disagreeing Actively
    Adaptive   Unadaptive   Not Sure
    1_____   2_____   3_____
N. Terminating Conversation
    Adaptive   Unadaptive   Not Sure
    1_____   2_____   3_____
O. Asking Why
    Adaptive   Unadaptive   Not Sure
    1_____   2_____   3_____
P. Making Requests
    Adaptive   Unadaptive   Not Sure
    1_____   2_____   3_____
Q. Saying No
    Adaptive   Unadaptive   Not Sure
    1_____   2_____   3_____

II. *Nonverbal Behavior*
    A. Postural Stance
        Adaptive   Unadaptive   Not Sure
        1_____   2_____   3_____
    B. Distance from People When Talking
        Adaptive   Unadaptive   Not Sure
        1_____   2_____   3_____
    C. Facial Expressions
        Adaptive   Unadaptive   Not Sure
        1_____   2_____   3_____
    D. Eye Contact
        Adaptive   Unadaptive   Not Sure
        1_____   2_____   3_____
    E. Hand and Other Body Movements
        Adaptive   Unadaptive   Not Sure
        1_____   2_____   3_____

Particular behavior(s) in need of assertive training. (Write on a separate sheet of paper, if more space is needed.)

Assertive Behavior Record Form

The Assertive Behavior Record Form is another means you can use to identify problem areas in your behavior. This form is designed to enable you to record and describe the specific situations in which you are unable to respond assertively. Each time you encounter such a situation, you record the date in column one. In column two, you describe the situation as clearly as you can, paying particular attention to how you felt when the incident occurred. In column three, you write in detail how *you would have liked to respond* if you had been able to behave assertively. Here is an example of a completed record form.

ASSERTIVE BEHAVIOR RECORD FORM

Date	Situation	Assertive Response
10/10	Waiting for my order to be taken at Dino's Restaurant. Waiter ignored me and served others who came after me. Felt hurt and angry.	Call waiter over, explain that I've been waiting for some time, and tell him that I feel I should be served before those who came after me.
10/15	John asked to borrow my tape recorder. Felt anxious and annoyed at John for asking, because he never returns what he borrows. Yet, I gave him the tape recorder, without saying a word about returning it promptly.	Talk to John and tell him "John, I'm afraid to loan you my tape recorder because I don't know when you'll return it. I'm still waiting for my camera and my tool kit. If you are sure that you can give it back to me at the end of the week, you may borrow it. But please remember that I need it back by Friday."
10/15	My secretary keeps interrupting me when I'm talking with clients. Today it was really embarrassing. I was furious.	Wait until the client has left. Call Marie into my office and explain that her habit embarrasses me and that from now on she should not disturb me when I'm in conference, unless there is an emergency.
10/18	Once again Tom attacked my opinion on politics and tried to force his views on me. This time his attack was pretty vicious. I felt very insulted, but I didn't say a word to him.	"Tom, this has to stop. Please respect my opinion on politics, as I respect yours. I'm tired of your attacks and of your trying to push your views on me. If you don't think you can keep from doing this, let's not discuss politics at all."
10/21	My friend Lynn always calls me fatso or tubby in front of our friends. I'm on the chubby side, and I feel very self-conscious about it. Today he called me tubby in front of my date. I could have punched him in the nose, but I kept quiet.	Tell Lynn that I know I'm overweight and I'm trying to stay on a diet. Explain that I'm self-conscious about my weight and that his calling me tubby in front of people makes me feel even more self-conscious and very uncomfortable. Ask him to stop referring to my weight, which is none of his business, in front of others.

Date	Situation	Assertive Response
10/22	My colleague Bob sloughs off on his work, and it reflects poorly on me. He's supposed to finish his weekly report on Monday afternoon but always hands it in on Tuesday or Wednesday. My report should be in on Monday afternoon, too, but I need his to complete mine. This week I didn't get his report till today—Thursday—and I was very upset and angry.	Talk to Bob and tell him "Bob, by not turning in your report on Monday, as you are supposed to, you cause me to be delinquent with my own report. I don't think this is fair. Please make sure that in the future you submit your report on time."
11/1	Every time I board a bus, I let everybody else get on first. It doesn't make any difference whether I get to the bus stop before or after the others; I always feel compelled to board last. This morning the bus was full, and I couldn't get on. I felt very silly and depressed.	Wait my turn to board the bus and make sure that I get on when my turn comes. If necessary, begin by making sure that I'm not the last to board (If I was not the last to arrive at the bus stop).

Now that you have had a chance to study the sample Assertive Behavior Record Form (ABRF), use the blank form below to keep a record of your behavior for the duration of the assertive-training period. (Additional blank forms are provided in Appendix B.) See if you can recall a situation you encountered today in which you think you could have behaved more assertively. What about yesterday or the day before? Surely there must have been situations that you could have handled in a more adaptive-assertive manner. Write the date of the incident in column one; give a brief description of the situation in column two; and in column three describe how you could have handled the situation more assertively. By keeping this record for a one-week period, you will be in a better position to identify your strengths and weaknesses and to keep track of your progress. (The ABRF will be discussed again in Chapter Six.)

Date	Situation	Assertive Response

Date	Situation	Assertive Response

Date	Situation	Assertive Response

Rathus Assertiveness Schedule

Another useful tool for assessing one's assertive (or nonassertive) behavior is the Rathus Assertiveness Schedule (RAS) by Rathus (1973a), presented below. To complete this schedule, assign a value to each statement by choosing from the code at the top of the scale the value number that describes you best. Write these value numbers in the blanks preceding the statements. To find out your score, sum the value numbers. (For statements followed by an asterisk, reverse the sign of the value number.) The following criteria should help you evaluate your score.

National norms for college and university students:
Average Score for Males: 12   Standard Deviation: 22
Average Score for Females: 7   Standard Deviation: 22

These norms are especially relevant for you if you are now or have recently been a college or university student. More generally, however, if your score on the RAS is 20 points or more below the average for your sex, it falls in the category of nonassertiveness. Neurotics tend to score significantly lower than normals on this scale (Rathus, personal communication).

RATHUS ASSERTIVENESS SCHEDULE

Directions: Using the code given below, indicate how characteristic or descriptive of you each of the following statements is.

+3   very characteristic, extremely descriptive
+2   rather characteristic, quite descriptive
+1   somewhat characteristic, slightly descriptive
−1   somewhat uncharacteristic, slightly nondescriptive
−2   rather uncharacteristic, quite nondescriptive
−3   very uncharacteristic, extremely nondescriptive

_____ 1. Most people seem to be more aggressive and assertive than I am.*
_____ 2. I have hesitated to make or accept dates because of "shyness."*
_____ 3. When the food served at a restaurant is not done to my satisfaction, I complain about it to the waiter or waitress.
_____ 4. I am careful to avoid hurting other people's feelings, even when I feel that I have been injured.*
_____ 5. If a salesman has gone to considerable trouble to show me merchandise that is not quite suitable, I have a difficult time in saying "No."*
_____ 6. When I am asked to do something, I insist upon knowing why.
_____ 7. There are times when I look for a good, vigorous argument.
_____ 8. I strive to get ahead as well as most people in my position.
_____ 9. To be honest, people often take advantage of me.*
_____ 10. I enjoy starting conversations with new acquaintances and strangers.
_____ 11. I often don't know what to say to attractive persons of the opposite sex.*
_____ 12. I will hesitate to make phone calls to business establishments and institutions.*
_____ 13. I would rather apply for a job or for admission to a college by writing letters than by going through with personal interviews.*

_____ 14. I find it embarrassing to return merchandise.*

_____ 15. If a close and respected relative were annoying me, I would smother my feelings rather than express my annoyance.*

_____ 16. I have avoided asking questions for fear of sounding stupid.*

_____ 17. During an argument I am sometimes afraid that I will get so upset that I will shake all over.*

_____ 18. If a famous and respected lecturer makes a statement that I think is incorrect, I will have the audience hear my point of view as well.

_____ 19. I avoid arguing over prices with clerks and salesmen.*

_____ 20. When I have done something important or worthwhile, I manage to let others know about it.

_____ 21. I am open and frank about my feelings.

_____ 22. If someone has been spreading false and bad stories about me, I see him (her) as soon as possible to "have a talk" about it.

_____ 23. I often have a hard time saying "No."*

_____ 24. I tend to bottle up my emotions rather than make a scene.*

_____ 25. I complain about poor service in a restaurant and elsewhere.

_____ 26. When I am given a compliment, I sometimes just don't know what to say.*

_____ 27. If a couple near me in a theatre or at a lecture were conversing rather loudly, I would ask them to be quiet or to take their conversation elsewhere.

_____ 28. Anyone attempting to push ahead of me in a line is in for a good battle.

_____ 29. I am quick to express an opinion.

_____ 30. There are times when I just can't say anything.*

---

*Reversed item.

From "A 30-Item Schedule for Assessing Assertive Behavior," by S.A. Rathus, *Behavior Therapy*, 1973, 4, 398–406. Copyright 1973 by Academic Press, Inc. Reprinted by permission.

Scales similar to the RAS are available for college students (Galassi, Delo, Galassi, & Bastein, 1974) and other adults (Gay, Hollandsworth, & Galassi, 1975).

How to Correctly Evaluate
One's Behavior

How do you determine whether your behavior is nonassertive, aggressive, or assertive? In clear-cut cases, in which you can easily see whether you "stood your ground" and asserted yourself, evaluating your own behavior is relatively easy; but not all cases are clear-cut, and sometimes you may find it difficult to judge. Being able to correctly identify and evaluate your behavior is very important; if you think that your responses are assertive when, in fact, they are nonassertive or aggressive, you may hinder your efforts to achieve a more adaptive style of interaction. This is, therefore, a challenging and important part of your assertive training.

In a series of audiotapes, Lazarus (1972) offers some very useful suggestions for correctly evaluating one's own behavior. Lazarus says that, when you are in doubt about how your behavior is coming across to others, you should simply put yourself in the position of an outside observer and then ask yourself how he or she would judge your behavior. The example Lazarus provides to illustrate his suggestion goes somewhat like this:

Suppose you are an executive and you are in your office with another person, when your secretary abruptly walks in, flings the morning mail on your desk, and strides out. How would it look to the other person if you (1) did nothing; (2) jumped up cursing and yelling at your secretary; (3) called her back and asked for an explanation of her behavior? It appears fairly obvious that, if you did nothing, the other person might think that you were weak, docile, ineffectual, and unable to stand up for yourself. If you blew up and related aggressively to the secretary, the other person might think that you were overreacting, harsh, and hostile. By calling your secretary back and asking if something was troubling her, the other person would be likely to think that you were effectively communicating your dissatisfaction and that you were seeking an explanation of her behavior.

The technique of asking yourself how an outside observer would judge your behavior is a good self-evaluation procedure. Whenever you find yourself in a situation in which you can choose among various possible responses, ask yourself how an outsider would judge each response, and then opt for the one that you feel would be judged as an assertive response. Granted, in most of our daily interactions we don't have the time and opportunity to engage in these evaluative exercises; but, as a general guideline, the use of the outside-observer technique provides a valuable perspective for judging one's behavior.

Lazarus's technique may be employed without enlisting the aid of others. Other methods you can use to evaluate your behavior require the cooperation of other people. The simplest, of course, is to just ask other people how your actions appear to them. This method is particularly useful as a confirmation of the objectivity of your self-evaluation. If you are undergoing assertive training under a therapist's guidance, the therapist will evaluate your behavior as you report it, give you feedback and instructions, and, more generally, oversee your assertion training.

You may receive feedback from other persons, too; your spouse, friends, and relatives are all good sources of information. Probably, the most effective feedback comes from the person with whom you are interacting at the time. If you have a question as to how you are coming across, ask the other person. "Do you feel that I'm infringing on your rights?" "Does my behavior strike you as aggressive?" and similar questions can provide the desired feedback. Of course, this technique, for one reason or another, may not be appropriate with everybody; but, if you are with people with whom you feel comfortable, try it.

Reality Testing

The term *reality testing* means simply checking your perception of your own behavior with some external source. This point was touched upon in the preceding section; here, we discuss in more detail how the individual undergoing assertive training can validate his or her perceptions by checking if they are congruent with those of others. This can be accomplished in a variety of ways.

Perhaps the most obvious way of determining the validity of how you perceive your behavior is simply for you to ask people how *they* perceive your behavior. This sounds simple enough, and in many cases it represents adequate reality testing. If you are interacting with someone and, for one reason or another, you feel that his responses are not those that you feel your behavior warrants, ask him whether he feels that your behavior is offensive. If he says yes, ask him what specifically in your behavior he finds offensive. It may be something quite simple, such as joking about his being overweight, in which case you may want to stop this behavior. But whatever he says, his response will tell you how you are coming across.

The individual in need of assertive training typically misperceives in the area of personal interactions. Because of his misperceptions, he may experience guilt, regret, and sorrow in situations that don't call at all for such reactions. Or he may experience anger and resentment, which, in turn, may make him ascribe similar feelings to the individual with whom he is interacting, thus creating a vicious circle. The ability to tactfully ask such questions as "Have I done anything to offend you?" is a useful interpersonal skill to develop. These questions are quite helpful in assertive training and serve as a good reality-testing procedure. A friend, a colleague, or any other observer may be used to check how one's behavior is perceived by others.

Cognitive Restructuring

The term *cognitive restructuring*, as used in this book, refers to the correcting or changing of one's thinking in regard to certain matters. Nonassertive or aggressive individuals often have faulty beliefs or attitudes that tend to maintain their unadaptive behavior. We noted earlier that values and attitudes of nonassertive people seem to be patterned after the slogan "The meek shall inherit the earth." Such values and attitudes make the development of assertive behavior fairly difficult. These individuals often believe that assertion is morally wrong. Cognitive restructuring involves the replacement of this approach with one that recognizes the merits and virtues of assertive behavior. It is essential that individuals seeking to develop assertive behavior be intellectually attuned to the merits of such behavior and that they firmly believe that it is to their benefit to develop more assertive response patterns. Guilt, reticence, or any other negative feeling should be disassociated from assertive training.

The aggressive individual, on the other hand, may equate aggressive behavior with strength and see anything less than aggression as a sign of weakness. This equally erroneous conception also needs to be changed before more appropriate assertive behavior can be developed. Wolpe (1973) reports that a feature many individuals in need of assertive training have in common is the belief that the rights of others are more important than their own—a belief that is the result of an early education overemphasizing social obligations.

> Before assertive training can begin, the patient must accept its reasonableness. Sometimes submission to the needs of others is bound up with the general philosophy that it is morally good to place the interests of others ahead of one's own. This is most often encountered in some devout Christians whose foremost emulation of Christ consists of turning the other cheek [p. 83].

Lazarus (1971), in stressing the importance of cognitive restructuring, contends:

> The bulk of therapeutic endeavors may be said to center around the correction of misconceptions. The people who consult us (professional therapists) tend to view innocuous events as extremely noxious and may disregard objectively noxious situations. Therapy often strives to show people how to separate subjective from objective dangers. Thereafter, the emphasis is on avoiding or coping with objectively hazardous events while ignoring the innocuous situations [p. 165].

As we said earlier, cognitive restructuring is aimed at getting the individual to see the value of assertive behavior. But cognitive restructuring alone is seldom sufficient for the development of assertive behavior; rather, it "sets the stage" by permitting the individual to be more receptive to behavioral change. The particular beliefs antagonistic to assertion are restructured to make them more conducive to the desired behavioral change.

One important point needs clarification. When one's behavior undergoes an overall change and becomes more assertive, changes in one's feelings or emotions will follow; that is, once beliefs counteracting assertive training are eliminated through cognitive restructuring, behavioral changes follow, and these changes are, in turn, followed by changes in feelings or emotions. Thus, once someone has come to believe in the moral virtue or personal advantage of assertion, specific behavioral procedures may be carried out.

The Case of Beverly

Beverly could not understand her chronic tension, headaches, and general discomfort. She went to a behavior therapist because she had been told by her physician that her problems were not physical in nature but mental. The behavior therapist soon realized that most of Beverly's "physical" complaints were the outcome of her total lack of assertiveness in interpersonal situations. He knew that, before attempting to change her behavior, he had to change her basic approach to assertiveness.

Beverly had been raised by very strict, "cold" parents, who firmly believed that one should be charitable and forgiving toward others but never toward oneself. The therapist spent several sessions challenging this belief. He pointed out to Beverly that it was her responsibility to stand up for herself, just as it was her fellow human beings' responsibility to stand up for themselves. He made Beverly see the difference between assertiveness and aggressiveness and discussed with her the negative aspects of both nonassertiveness and aggressiveness. Beverly began to see the problem that some of her beliefs and attitudes presented and finally realized that these very beliefs and attitudes were largely responsible for her lack of assertiveness. This understanding, and the subsequent change in attitudes, made it possible for Beverly to approach assertive training with enthusiasm and to be ready for the application of specific behavioral techniques.

Beverly's case illustrates the value of cognitive restructuring in the development of assertive training and the importance attached in behavior therapy to the awareness of one's mental activities. On the other hand, as we said earlier, cognitive restructuring is only a phase of behavior therapy, whose goal is not that of simply changing ideas, feelings, and beliefs but of actually modifying behavior.

Suggested Reading

Ciminero, A. R., Calhoun, K. S., & Adams, H. E. (Eds.). *Handbook of behavioral assessment.* New York: John Wiley & Sons, in press.

Chapter Five / Assertive verbal and nonverbal behavior

Topic Overview

I. Verbal behavior is essentially what sets humans apart from other primates.

II. The verbal skills that assertive training seeks to improve are:
  1. Initiating conversations
  2. Maintaining control of conversations
  3. Extemporaneous talking
  4. Expressing emotions
  5. Feeling talk and emotional honesty
  6. Expressing positive feelings
     a. Paying compliments
     b. Expressing affection
     c. Expressing empathy
     d. Giving and encouraging greetings
  7. Talking about oneself
  8. Using the personal pronoun "I"
  9. Accepting compliments
  10. Disagreeing passively and actively
  11. Asking why
  12. Making requests
  13. Saying no
  14. Terminating conversations
  15. Voice volume
  16. Speech fluency

III. Nonverbal behavior reflects an attitude; it communicates to others how we view ourselves and the particular behavior in which we are engaging.

IV. Nonverbal behaviors that can be improved with assertive training are:
   1. Physical distance when interacting
   2. Postural stance
   3. Unrelated hand and other body movements
   4. Eye contact
   5. Facial talk

We come now to a discussion of the actual development of assertive behavior. In this chapter, the focus is on the skills that can be developed without necessarily receiving professional direction. It should be noted that some of these skills are discussed again in Chapter Six—this time as behavioral procedures to be developed under a therapist's guidance.

After reading the preceding chapters, which provided a framework for identifying specific assertive behavioral deficiencies and some guidance on how to correct them, you may have come to the conclusion that you are not in need of assertive training. Even so, the topics discussed in this and in the following chapter may prove beneficial to you by helping you change certain aspects of your behavior that you feel could be improved.

Assertive Verbal Behavior

We begin with a discussion of verbal behavior. Keep in mind that, although assertive verbal behavior and assertive nonverbal behavior are discussed separately for greater clarity, in actuality the two can hardly be separated, since the manner in which something is asserted is dependent on both the verbal and the nonverbal components of behavior.

Although recent research indicates that some animals can "talk," or at least communicate with each other at a rudimentary level, verbal skills are essentially what sets humans apart from the other primates. By talking, we communicate our feelings, thoughts, and desires and work toward achieving our goals. Of course, mere verbal adeptness—even exceptional adeptness—is not a guarantee of adequate behavioral adjustment in general or of assertiveness in particular. There are gifted individuals who are able to effectively communicate precisely what they wish to say and yet do not behave assertively. The important point is *how* one uses one's verbal skills. For one, verbal skills should not be used to abuse others, as we saw in the example of Nancy's aggressive behavior, cited in Chapter Four; on the other hand, assertive verbal behavior is necessary under certain circumstances, and adequate verbal skills, if used assertively, are very important in achieving and maintaining an adequate behavioral adjustment.

We are all familiar with individuals who lack assertive verbal skills. Instead of speaking, they whisper; their speech has no fluency; and they find it very hard to initiate a conversation. These individuals need to learn to develop more adequate and efficient verbal skills—in other words, more assertive verbal behavior.

Initiating Conversations

The ability to initiate conversations is a very important verbal skill—and one of the most difficult for nonassertive and aggressive individuals to master. For the nonassertive, a lack of this skill is a constant source of conflict and anxiety; for the aggressive, a source of frustration often expressed in aggressive and obnoxious behavior that offends and turns people off.

The individual concerned with developing assertive behavior must learn how to appropriately approach people and initiate conversations. Learning these skills, like learning most other skills, is a gradual process. A good way to start is by considering various ways of initiating conversations. Attention should be directed more to the act of initiating the conversation than to the content of the conversation, although what is said should, of course, be inoffensive and of some interest to other people. But the important point here is the actual initiation of the conversation.

Practice may begin with friends and relatives and later include other people. Every time you succeed in initiating a conversation, tell yourself "Very good!"; this will provide effective reinforcement. In order to initiate a conversation, you must, of course, have something to say that can offer useful openings. A thorough reading of the daily newspaper can provide you with many bits of information that you can use to initiate conversations. For example, "Ed, did you read in this morning's paper about the guy who won $64,000 on a sweepstake ticket he found in the subway?" or "The review of Fellini's last movie in the *Herald* is very good. Have you seen that movie?" and so on. Often we don't realize that we are not alone in finding it difficult to initiate conversations; many other people cannot do it as easily as they would like to. Consequently, when people meet and someone does break the ice by initiating a conversation, all present feel relieved and are generally eager to seize the opportunity for joining in.

With time and practice, you will find it easier and easier to initiate a conversation. You can speed your progress by giving yourself "homework assignments" requiring that you initiate a certain number of conversations each week.

Maintaining Control of Conversations

The skill of maintaining control of conversations is closely related to that of initiating conversations, but often it is a bit more difficult. The reason is simply that the other participants may feel that they have something to contribute to the ongoing conversation and are impatient to do so. This often results in people interrupting—at times quite rudely—someone who is talking. For many of us this is not a problem; but for nonassertive individuals, being interrupted is like a slap in the face and, we may add, a good opportunity for surrendering the role of talking. Being interrupted makes nonassertive individuals feel that what they are saying is trivial or that they are not "entitled" to speak. It is almost a reflex response on their part that, whenever someone interrupts them, they have to stop talking and listen to the other person. They greet being interrupted with mixed feelings. On the one hand, they share in the natural desire of wanting to make their point; on the other hand, they welcome the opportunity for letting someone else carry the conversation. And their reticence in asserting themselves makes it virtually impossible for them to regain control of the conversation after they have been interrupted. In assertive training, nonassertive individuals practice ways that permit them to maintain control of a conversation and complete their statements once they have been interrupted.

One way of maintaining control while talking is simply to *amplify*—to speak in a louder voice. If amplification does not work, you can try waiting until the person who interrupted you stops talking and then return to what you were saying when you were interrupted, ignoring what the other person said. Another (and more assertive) response would be to come right out and ask the other person if he or she would mind waiting until you finished talking before making his or her statement.

Extemporaneous Talking

This is perhaps the area in which many nonassertive individuals experience the greatest difficulty. Extemporaneous talking refers to saying something on the spur of the moment, so to speak. It is talking without being called upon—the volunteering of unsolicited comments, critical or otherwise. It may be expressing feelings, giving information, or just relating an experience or describing a situation. The essential point is that it is the speaker who elects to talk, without waiting to be asked. Extemporaneous talking requires spontaneity and freedom from fear, hesitancies, and other hindrances; therefore, nonassertive individuals find it particularly difficult to engage in this kind of talking, since they lack the very freedom that this behavior requires. We said "behavior," because extemporaneous talking, too, is a behavior—a verbal one, but still a behavior—and thus can be developed with practice.

Deficiency in the skill of extemporaneous talking is most evident in group settings, and both aggressive and nonassertive individuals are likely to show this deficiency. Aggressive people tend to dominate or attempt to dominate by forcing themselves upon the other group members; they inappropriately interrupt to interject their views, in disregard of the rights of others. Although aggressive individuals, too, need to change their behavior into a more adaptive one, our attention here will be directed mostly toward nonassertive individuals, for they are, in our opinion, those who are in greater need of assistance.

If you are a nonassertive individual and thus more of a listener than a talker, in order to master the skill of extemporaneous speaking, you need to talk more. How? By just talking more! Start by speaking for graduated periods of 10, 15, 30, to 45 seconds. Talk to your spouse, to a friend, or even to yourself; if you are receiving professional assistance, you may, of course, talk to your therapist. The important point is that you get experience in speaking for longer and longer periods of time. If you cannot manage to talk for the periods suggested, even reading aloud is a useful activity. The motor skills of correct breathing, pronunciation, and articulation involved in speaking aloud need to be practiced, and reading aloud gives you the practice you need. Start by reading aloud for, say, five minutes, and gradually increase your practice to longer periods of time. Then, or before if you wish, start practicing speaking extemporaneously for graduated periods of time, as suggested above. Remember, for the purpose of practicing, it doesn't really matter what you say; the important point is that you practice talking extemporaneously for extended periods of time. With practice, extemporaneous talking will become easier and easier, especially if you receive encouragement and support from others, and at one point you will realize that you have truly mastered the skills involved in extemporaneous speaking—skills that will eventually become a part of your assertive behavioral repertoire.

One word of caution before leaving the topic of extemporaneous speaking: excessive talking not only is *not* the goal of this approach but is a very undesirable behavior, at odds with the practice we have been discussing, which is aimed at developing the ability to express your views appropriately and comfortably.

Expressing Emotions

Nonassertive individuals are almost incapable of expressing anger, resentment, hostility, and similar feelings, since they have spent years controlling and suppressing these emotions. The effects of contained emotions are often deleterious to the body as well as the spirit. The most obvious of these effects is increasing frustration, which may find expression in totally inappropriate responses. It is not all that rare for the nonassertive individual to suddenly explode violently and untimely, often with unfortunate (and at times even dramatic) consequences. We are all familiar with newspaper stories about a "nice quiet boy" suddenly going berserk and shooting people at random. More common than these dramatic cases, however, are those of people who, although not necessarily overly inhibited, have kept from adequately expressing their negative emotions, such as resentment and anger, all their lives. These emotions grow and grow, until they suddenly burst out, often inappropriately.

Screaming, yelling, or cursing will not produce assertive behavior, nor will it by itself even come anywhere near producing such behavior. But it will be of value in unlocking and venting certain emotions, probably for the first time in a long while. Screaming, yelling, and cursing are behaviors—skills that can be developed. The consequence of these motor acts is a feeling of release for having "let it all out," which may become reinforcing to the nonassertive individual. Besides enjoying these beneficial aspects of the practiced expression of emotions, the individual is also developing a new skill—the skill of expressing his feelings. In general, once it has served its function of letting the individual "loosen up," thus facilitating his acquisition of assertive responses, the overexpression common during the initial phase of assertive training gradually gives way to more balanced and appropriate expressions of emotions.

Although it may be difficult to induce nonassertive individuals to yell or scream, an effort should be made to encourage them to try it. Then yelling may be gradually reduced to cursing and other forms of verbal aggression at a normal voice level. At this point, the individual begins to realize that his goal is not to develop aggressiveness but assertiveness.

It should be clear from our discussion that one of the goals of assertive training is affective reeducation—learning to replace anxiety responses with the feelings of confidence and satisfaction that derive from the assertive handling of interpersonal situations. This reeducation process may involve, as we have seen, evolving from a nonassertive to an aggressive and finally to an assertive mode of interaction.

Feeling Talk and Emotional Honesty

Salter (1949) said that individuals in need of assertive training are emotionally dishonest because they unnecessarily hide their true feelings. And it is not just the hostile or assertive feelings that are being hidden but other emotions as well.

Nonassertive people who have great difficulty expressing honestly their feelings play a perpetual guessing game of "reading" the expressions of others and slanting their behavior accordingly, expressing what they feel will please the listener. They seldom take stands, make bland statements, are perennially asking questions instead of making positive declarations, and generally appear weak and indecisive; in sum, they are poor and boring talkers. Since they are trying to give what they believe others want to hear rather than what they themselves feel, they inevitably fail to communicate effectively. These individuals have difficulty speaking for sustained periods of time and are afraid of being interrupted; therefore, they tend to encapsulate what they want to say in a few cryptic statements devoid of any feeling, often inadvertently blurted out. This, too, contributes to these people's failure to communicate effectively.

Being able to honestly express our feelings is a tremendously rewarding and enriching talent; it makes us feel good, and this, in return, is reinforcing and tends to increase the incidence of our expressing our true feelings. One of the goals of assertive training is to assist the individual to develop this talent and gradually learn to add emotional flavor to his talk. Salter (1949, pp. 96–97) provides several examples of feeling talk, and here are some of them.

Feeling-Talk Remarks	Feelings Being Expressed
I like soup.	Like
I hate parsnips.	Dislike
I don't like that person.	Dislike
You did a marvelous job, Miss Jones.	Praise
That hat really becomes you.	Praise
I cried when he came home safely.	Relief
Excuse me, but I was here first.	Complaint
I can hardly wait until he gets here.	Impatience
What a wonderful time we had!	Enjoyment
I cleaned out the poker game.	Self-praise
It was the most extraordinary thing I had seen in a long time.	Amazement
You don't expect me to believe that, do you?	Skepticism
I'm just dying to meet him.	Anticipation
There's nothing to it. I'll take care of it right away.	Confidence
I think the dessert was a mistake.	Regret
Good grief, I feel terrible about this.	Anguish
Today is Friday. The week went fast.	Surprise*

Individuals concerned with the development of assertive behavior should start including feeling talk in their conversations and be alert to every opportunity to practice it. Congratulating themselves when they succeed in adequately expressing their feelings is a useful and reinforcing procedure.

Expressing Positive Feelings

Several writers have been concerned with the expression of positive assertiveness. For example, Wolpe (1969) has stressed the distinction between "hostile" and "commendatory" assertion, and Lazarus (1971) has stated that most definitions of assertion do not include the expression of positive feelings, such as appreciation, affection, empathy, and understanding.

*From *Conditioned Reflex Therapy*, by Andrew Salter. Copyright 1949, 1961 by Andrew Salter. Reprinted by permission.

Eisler, Hersen, Miller, and Blanchard (1975) noted that until now most research studies have dealt mainly with the narrower definition of assertion, which they refer to as hostile assertion, and have failed to consider the positive forms of assertion. Expression of positive feelings (positive assertion), according to Eisler and his colleagues, is an integral part of assertive training.

Being able to communicate affection, empathy, or admiration for someone is an important component of an overall adaptive behavioral repertoire. This is not to say that sometimes an assertive response, although legitimate in terms of the situation, may not border on aggression. And yet, even in such instances, assertion can be positive, if nothing else by allowing the other individual an opportunity to save face. Tact and diplomacy are not incompatible with assertion. The goal of assertive training is not, in general, "turning others on" to us; but establishing satisfactory interpersonal relationships is certainly one of the goals we try to achieve. Positive assertion—the expression of positive feelings such as appreciation, affection, empathy, and understanding—can go a long way in helping us achieve that goal.

Paying Compliments

This behavioral skill requires that you be sincere—at least to a point; in other words, do not praise something you dislike. What you want is to be able, when you see something that impresses you favorably, to express your positive feelings, without going to extremes either by showering compliments on people or by being overenthusiastic. Suppose, for example, that one of your coworkers has bought a new suit, which looks very good on him. Saying something like "Well, George, that suit really looks good on you!" is both honest, because it reflects your feelings, and good for your relationship with George.

Developing the ability to pay compliments is not too difficult a task. It is something that you can practice without the aid of a therapist, and, if you use it judiciously, it generally permits you to achieve a more adaptive interactional style.

Expressing Affection

Perhaps because of the real or presumed risk of rejection, expressing affection is difficult for many of us all or some of the time. It is undeniable that someone to whom you express affection may not respond in the way you anticipated or hoped. The secret, if there is one, in developing this skill is to think of your goal as being the mere expression of the affection and not its effect. We don't claim that this is an easy approach, but it does permit you to engage in a fairly adaptive behavior and, at the same time, it minimizes your concern over its consequences. It should also be kept in mind that most people respond positively to sincere expressions of affection; it is realistic, therefore, to assume that, when you express affection to someone, the person is likely to respond favorably.

Expressing Empathy

Empathy refers to the ability to subjectively experience or participate in another person's ideas or feelings and to resonate to another's emotional state or attitude. In assertive training, individuals who would like to express their empathy to another person but are inhibited from doing so are encouraged to let themselves experience empathy and to try to express their feelings. If, after listening to a friend relate an upsetting experience, you begin to really know how he feels, tell him, share your feelings with him. When you do so, you show empathy.

Greeting Talk

This term refers to the social behavior of exchanging greetings with others. Are you someone who seldom or never gives a greeting and who unenthusiastically responds to greetings from others? Ask yourself how a cheerful and interested greeting from another affects you. It is likely that, like most of us, you tend to respond positively to such a greeting. The ability to successfully engage in greeting behavior is a good verbal assertive skill to develop.

Talking about Oneself

Often individuals in need of assertive training have developed the pattern of not talking about themselves. Because of excessive modesty or shyness, they very seldom, if ever, engage in the behavior of talking about themselves. Assertive training involves, among other things, helping individuals develop the habit of talking about themselves and replacing feelings of excessive modesty and shyness with feelings of self-confidence and outgoingness.

To develop the habit of talking about yourself, you should begin by doing some homework that requires you to talk about yourself for a certain period of time at least once a day. During these periods of practice, you should briefly monopolize the conversation to talk about yourself—for example, to relate something that happened to you and that you handled successfully. Here, too, what you say is not as important as the fact that you talk about it, thus gradually developing the behavior of talking about yourself. Needless to say, it is essential that you fully appreciate the value of the behavior in question.

Using the Personal Pronoun "I"

Many nonassertive individuals tend to avoid the use of the personal pronoun "I," as Salter (1949) remarked in his early work. Because of excessive modesty or, perhaps, fear of identifying themselves with their beliefs, these individuals find using "I" very difficult. Conversely, many aggressive or overassertive people may use "I" too much.

Here, too, as in all the aspects of behavior discussed in this book, the goal of assertive training is to develop an appropriate and balanced pattern. If you are not using the pronoun "I" enough, practice by making a point, every time you are discussing your beliefs, feelings, and desires, to identify with them by saying "I believe," "I feel," "I wish," and so on. Soon this verbal skill—because this, too, is a verbal skill—will become part of your increasingly assertive behavioral repertoire.

Accepting Compliments

Learning to accept compliments, to agree gracefully with something positive that is said about you, is another response pattern you may need to develop. If you are like many of us who have acquired an almost reflex habit of responding to compliments by disagreeing with them, then you must learn to change this habit and accept compliments—at least certain compliments—by gracefully agreeing with them. When you receive a compliment that sounds sincere, instead of saying "Oh, it's nothing," try to say "Why, yes, thank you. I feel the same!" At first, you may feel pretty awkward, even foolish, but eventually you will find that accepting compliments has become a very natural response for you.

Disagreeing Passively and Actively

Many nonassertive individuals have a tendency to agree with people in general and with opinionated people in particular to avoid an open difference of opinion. In assertive training, you learn to develop alternative responses to indiscriminate agreement.

You may disagree passively by simply not making a statement of agreement with something someone said. Instead of agreeing, you may say nothing or perhaps even change the topic of conversation. The skill of passive disagreement can be developed fairly easily. Once you have mastered it, you may be ready to engage in active disagreement—coming right out and stating that you don't agree with something someone said. Like all other assertive skills, active disagreement should be developed gradually. You should practice disagreeing on minor issues that are devoid of emotional content and gradually move on to more heated topics. The important thing is that each little act of active disagreement be followed by rewarding consequences. This is possible only when disagreement is assertive and *not* aggressive. In fact, aggressive individuals need as much as nonassertive people to develop a viable and satisfactory style of disagreeing. Assertive training will aim at eliminating their aggressive—and, therefore, nonproductive—mode and at developing, instead, a more appropriate assertive approach. If, for example, someone's manner of disagreeing is that of launching a vitriolic attack on the speaker, the person must, first of all, come to realize that this behavior is unadaptive and needs to be replaced (cognitive restructuring) and then follow with the gradual implementation of assertive alternatives.

Asking Why

Another problem individuals in need of assertive training may have is an inability to ask for explanations. They seem to feel that asking why is an offensive act, or they may actually be afraid of asking why and therefore inhibit the need to do so. As a consequence, these people are likely to go along with any request that is made of them, no matter how unreasonable. Assertive training encourages you to develop the habit of asking why. It makes clear to you that it is important (and legitimate) that you ask for explanations, and it provides encouragement and support for each effort you make in that direction. You are taught how to word your request for an explanation in different ways, depending on the situation, and you also practice the art of simply asking why. As a start, if the repair bill for your car is 50% higher than the estimate, ask why!

Making Requests

The nonassertive individual may find making requests very difficult; the aggressive individual, too easy. One hardly ever asks for anything; the other often asks for too much. Here, too, the goal is a harmonious balance that permits the person to make appropriate and legitimate requests. What are legitimate requests? The answer to this question depends, of course, on the situational context. If, for example, your neighbor keeps borrowing your tools but seldom returns them, it would certainly be legitimate for you to request that he do so. If, on several occasions, your friend Liza has asked you to feed her cat while she was away and now that you are going to be out of town you ask that she feed your cat, you are making a legitimate request. But keep in mind that a request can be legitimate even though you do not feel someone is "beholden" to you because you have done favors to that person. The fact of the matter is that it is perfectly all right to make *reasonable* requests of others! Incidentally, others may deny your request without even offering an explanation; but, for the purpose of developing assertive behavior, the important thing is that you learn to make appropriate, reasonable requests and that you view doing so as perfectly legitimate.

This behavior, as all the others we have discussed, should be developed gradually. Begin by making very minor requests of people who you believe will honor your requests, and gradually move to situations that involve more assertive behavior. Be prepared for refusals, and do not be dismayed.

Saying No

Can you come right out and say no to someone? Of course, this question is difficult to answer without knowing the situation in which you would have to do so. But suppose that you find yourself in a situation in which you feel that saying no and nothing more is a very appropriate behavior. Can you then say no? For many of us, simply saying no is difficult; we believe we have to qualify what we say and offer elaborate justifications; furthermore, we generally feel quite uncomfortable. And yet there are situations—we all encounter them—in which a simple, direct no is the most appropriate behavior. If you are one of those who find it difficult to say no, you need to develop this skill, so that, when the situations we have been discussing do arise, you will be able to respond assertively.

Aggressive individuals, on the other hand, say no without offering any reasons for it, even when the circumstances dictate that they do so. They, too, need to modify their behavior so they can say no assertively rather than aggressively.

Terminating Conversations

Terminating conversations, just like initiating them, can prove very difficult for the nonassertive individual. For most people, terminating a conversation simply means making a closing statement and leaving; not so for nonassertive people. They are at a loss as to how to go about it; typically, they tend to overstay, and even the most rewarding conversation ends up dwindling to an almost aversive level. The reason for this behavior is that to the nonassertive individual saying goodbye or making some kind of closing statement is an emotionally tinged act akin to assertion and thus inhibited. By "emotionally tinged" we mean that the behavior of the nonassertive individual is an emotional response to fear—fear of offending the person or persons with whom he is talking. As a result, he keeps hanging around long past the appropriate time to take his leave.

In assertive training, you are directed toward developing the skill of terminating conversations. This skill involves a good balance of tact and assertiveness and results in effective and appropriate closing statements—statements you make to indicate to the people with whom you are talking that you are getting ready to terminate the conversation. Ideally, a closing statement should convey the feeling that you have enjoyed the conversation; abruptly ending and walking away is therefore not an appropriate way of terminating a conversation! Most people would regard it as an offensive, even aggressive, act, and your popularity would hardly benefit from it. Smooth, tactful closing statements, such as those in the examples below, should be incorporated into your behavioral repertoire.

Situation	*Closing Statement*
You are visiting at Don's house. You feel you have stayed long enough and are ready to leave.	"Well, Don, I really enjoyed the evening, but now I must go. I look forward to seeing you again soon."
You are talking with a colleague. You must leave because you have an appointment.	"I enjoyed talking with you and would love to continue, but I have an appointment and must leave now."
You have received a sales pitch for a home fire alarm.	"Thank you for your time and effort, but I am definitely not interested in buying a fire alarm."

Voice Volume

How loudly or softly we speak influences how we perceive ourselves as well as how others perceive us. In general, and exceptions notwithstanding, someone who speaks in a very soft, "faint" voice tends to be perceived as shy and nonassertive, and someone who speaks too loudly, as aggressive and obstreperous. Both need to change the volume of their voices as part of their assertiveness program.

How loudly should you speak? If, when you talk, people tend to tune you out and not notice you because they can't hear what you are saying or, conversely, they tend to be turned off because you make too much noise, you need to attend to the loudness of your voice. After you have studied the volume of your voice (a tape recorder may be of great help), begin to modify your verbal behavior to achieve adequate loudness. By adequate loudness we usually mean a volume of voice that permits the person to be easily heard in a normal conversation. Keep in mind, though, that sometimes we compete with surrounding noises or with other people talking. If you are not talking loud enough, you may, for example, ask someone to stand ten feet away and, as you practice speaking, tell you if he or she has any difficulty hearing and understanding you. If so, keep practicing until the person can hear you clearly. If you think that you speak too loudly, practice in the same way making an effort to lower your voice, so that the individual standing ten feet away can receive your message clearly and comfortably.

The following are exercises to achieve and maintain adequate voice volume. Practice them several times, until you feel that you are speaking in an adequately loud voice.

1. Initiate an "ah" in a tone which is barely audible, gradually increasing the loudness of the "ah" until it is louder than your usual conversational voice, and then reduce the loudness until the tone is again barely audible. Do not change the pitch or force the length of exhalation beyond a point of comfort.

2. Count from one to five, increasing the loudness on each number. Begin with a barely audible "one" and end with a "five" which can easily be heard across a 40-foot room.

3. Count to seven, increasing the loudness up to four and then decreasing the loudness from five through seven. Maintain the same pitch level throughout the count.

4. Say each of the following phrases or sentences three times, increasing the loudness from a normal conversational level to one which can easily be heard across a 40-foot room.
   a. I'll go!
   b. Come back!
   c. Please!
   d. No!
   e. I won't!
   f. Enough!
   g. Who's there?

5. Read each of the following sentences, first in an ordinary conversational tone and then as if you were trying to address a person in the tenth row of a crowded room.
   a. I'll go in a few minutes.
   b. The time is now.
   c. I'll say this for the last time.
   d. Listen, if you wish to understand.
   e. Are you John Jones?*

Speech Fluency

Speech fluency refers to the ability to speak easily and expressively. Fluent speech does not come easily to many of us but can be developed with practice. One of the goals of verbal assertive training is the development of fluent speech, a speech free of long, awkward pauses, of repetitions, hesitations, and use of expletives such as "oh," "uhm," and "ah." If you want to know how fluent your speech is, ask yourself these questions:

1. Is my speech pleasant to hear?
2. Do I communicate effectively, both from the point of view of content and from that of feeling?
3. Does my speech reflect me as I am?
4. How would I respond to someone whose speech was like mine?

Your answers to these questions will dictate the remediation procedures (if any) you need. If you have a tape recorder, monitor your behavior by recording a typical interaction. Playing back this tape may reveal some areas in which you need to develop more fluency.

Assertive Nonverbal Behavior

Nonverbal behavior, like other forms of behavior, reflects an attitude. It communicates to others how we view ourselves and the particular behavior in which we are engaging and, therefore, if we are assertive or nonassertive individuals. Stoop shoulders, hand wringing, lowered head, and averted eyes are more likely to communicate insecurity, meekness, timidity, possibly guilt or anxiety than confidence and assurance, and they all typify nonassertive nonverbal behavior.

Assertive nonverbal behavior can be developed by attending to how we appear to others and by modifying all the postures described above—standing straight with shoulders back, head raised, hands stretched out at one's sides in a relaxed, confident manner, and maintaining adequate eye contact with the person(s) with whom we are interacting.

*These exercises are taken from *The Improvement of Voice and Diction*, by J. Eisenson. Copyright © 1958 by Macmillan Publishing Co., Inc. Reprinted by permission.

Physical Distance When Interacting

When interacting with others, there is a culturally defined physical distance that one is expected to maintain. Reducing this distance may make the other person uncomfortable, and he or she may literally back away. Standing too far away, as some nonassertive individuals do, may communicate timidity and insecurity—even a fear of contact. Observe other people interacting. How close do they stand? What does the distance they maintain with others indicate? You can learn a great deal by this practice of observation and, if necessary, modify your own behavior accordingly.

Postural Stance

Our posture tells a great deal about us. A straight, erect posture connotes confidence and pride, while a stoop-shouldered, head-lowered posture indicates the opposite. If your posture is not as you think it should be, work at it; make an effort to stand straight, with shoulders back and head raised.

Unrelated Hand and Other Body Movements

Often nonassertive individuals develop excessive and/or unrelated hand and other body movements. This is the case, for example, with someone who, while talking, nervously drums his fingers on his thigh and shifts his weight from foot to foot. Attend to your own behavior. Do you engage in these and other unrelated body movements while you are interacting with others? If you do, concentrate on eliminating or reducing the inappropriate behavior.

Eye Contact

Nonassertive individuals are likely to experience anxiety when interacting with people. Consequently, they often don't maintain adequate eye contact and tend to look away when talking with others. It is almost as if eye contact represented some kind of confrontation requiring an act of assertion, and, since assertiveness is what these individuals lack, they tend to minimize eye contact and, therefore, the opportunities for asserting themselves.

If you are deficient in this skill, you should monitor your behavior and conscientiously practice maintaining eye contact whenever possible. This practice can be effectively carried out every time you interact with someone. Like the other skills discussed earlier, maintaining adequate eye contact must be developed gradually and reinforced as much as possible. Therefore, it is suggested that at first you practice maintaining eye contact with people you feel comfortable with, such as your spouse and your friends, and then try it with others.

Facial Talk

Facial talk (Salter, 1949) refers to facial expressions of emotions. Many individuals hide their emotions behind a constant mask, their faces never showing any emotions. This is particularly common among nonassertive individuals. They seldom smile, hardly ever grimace or grit their teeth, and rarely furrow their brows or arch their eyebrows; in other words, they don't engage in facial talk.

Part of assertive training consists in helping you to develop facial talk and thus more effectively communicate your feelings. If you are happy, say it and show it with a big smile. If you are angry, say it and let your face show it. Like all other forms of assertive behavior we have discussed, facial talk is developed by practice. Often the practice begins with overexpression—that is, with exaggerated facial expressions. If you are angry, you are encouraged to growl, squint your eyes, and furrow your brows. This will let you know what anger feels like when you let your face express it. Do the same with all the other emotions you feel; this will give you excellent practice in overexpression. Later, you can start toning down your expressions until they are appropriately assertive; you will have, of course, to enlist the aid of others to give you feedback as to how you are coming across. With continued practice, you will find that facial talk helps you communicate more effectively your feelings.

Smiling is a behavior that some individuals in need of assertive training engage in rarely. If you are one of them, begin by practicing in front of a mirror and noticing the difference that smile makes. Next, practice smiling as you interact with people you feel at ease with. Then, over time, gradually increase your smiling behavior until you have developed the ability to easily and comfortably smile whenever you feel it natural to do so.

Chapter Six / Behavioral procedures

Topic Overview

I. A review of the research conducted on various techniques used in assertive training to develop verbal and nonverbal skills

II. Behavioral procedures most commonly used in therapist-directed assertive training
1. Behavioral rehearsal and role playing
2. Modeling
3. Covert conditioning techniques
   a. Covert reinforcement
   b. Covert sensitization
   c. Covert modeling
4. Reinforcement
   a. Self-reinforcement
   b. Therapist-administered reinforcement
   c. Reinforcement by significant others
5. Information giving, coaching, and homework
6. Use of video- and audiotapes
7. Relaxation training

III. Development of positive assertion and a look at some situational determinants of assertive behavior

IV. Use of the Assertive Behavior Record Form (ABRF)

This chapter discusses the specific behavioral procedures that are used in assertive training and presents some of the research dealing with these procedures. Some nonprofessional readers might find parts of this and the following chapter somewhat too technically oriented. We hope that these readers will bear with us, keeping in mind that these two chapters relate to techniques used in assertive training under a therapist's guidance and are, therefore, directed especially to professionals.

We shall begin with a brief review of the research conducted on various techniques used in assertive training to develop verbal and nonverbal skills.

Developing Verbal Skills

Rathus (1972) indicated that verbal and nonverbal skills can be developed by group assertive training. He substantiated his statement with the results of an experiment conducted with 57 volunteers at a women's college. The subjects were randomly assigned to one of three groups: (1) assertive training, (2) group discussion of fears and related social problems, such as child-rearing practices leading to feelings of guilt, and (3) no treatment (control). The assertive-training subjects met with the experimenter in groups of six once a week for seven weeks. The first session was devoted to a discussion of the rationale for assertion. Treatment itself consisted of engaging in the following nine types of assertive behavior:[1]

1. *Assertive talk.* Subjects were told not to let others take advantage of them, to demand their rights, to insist that they be treated with fairness and justice. Examples: "I was here first." "Excuse me, but I have to be somewhere else in ten minutes." "Please turn off the radio; I have to study."

2. *Feeling talk.* Subjects were to express their likes and dislikes with spontaneity, to be open and frank about their feelings, to answer questions honestly, and to avoid bottling up emotions. Examples: "What a marvelous shirt!" "I am so sick of that man!" "Since you ask, I think the other outfit looked much better on you." "I think the film was trite; I really don't care what the critics thought."

3. *Greeting talk.* Subjects were to be outgoing and friendly with persons they wished to know better. They were not to avoid people because of shyness and be mistaken as snobbish. They were to smile brightly at people, to have little things prepared to say. Examples: "Hi, how are you?" "I haven't seen you in months." "What are you doing with yourself these days?" "Are you taking any good courses?" "What's happening with so and so?" "What do you think of___?"

4. *Disagreeing passively and actively.* Subjects were not to pretend to agree with opinionated people for the sake of "keeping the peace." They were to avoid

[1]Many of these tasks are derived from the "excitatory" exercises described by Salter (1949, pp. 97–103).

nodding in agreement, smiling encouragingly, and paying close attention. They were to change topics, look away, leave, or, when sure of their ground, counterattack emotionally.

5. *Asking why.* Subjects were to consider reasonable suggestions from others, but not to be ordered about at anybody's whim. When asked to do something that did not sound reasonable or enjoyable by a person in power or authority, they were to ask why they should comply and not settle for less than a convincing explanation.

6. *Talking about oneself.* Subjects were to let others know when they had done something enjoyable or worthwhile. They were to relate their experiences and "monopolize" a reasonable proportion of the conversations they entered.

7. *Agreeing with compliments.* When they felt a compliment was sincere, subjects were never to derogate themselves by saying, for example, "Oh, it's nothing." At the very least, they were to smile and say, "Thank you." They were also to reward the complimenter from time to time by smiling and saying something like "Why, thank you. That's an awfully nice thing to say. I appreciate it." Or, when it would not appear awkward, they were to extend the compliment. For instance, if told "That's a pretty sweater," they might respond "Why, thank you. I'm just in love with the color; I had a hard time finding it."

8. *Avoiding justifying opinions.* Subjects were not to be bullheaded in conversations, but they were to avoid attempting to justify themselves to antagonists who were overly pedantic and more concerned with dominating the social interaction than seeking truth. To such people they might say "Sorry, but I remembered an appointment." "Are you always so disagreeable?" "Winning arguments is awfully important to you, isn't it?" or "You seem to have a terrible time changing your mind. Doesn't that prevent you from learning new things?"

9. *Looking people in the eye.* Subjects were not to avoid the gaze of others. When they argued, expressed an opinion, paid a compliment, or greeted someone, they were to look him directly and continuously in the eye.*

The results of this experiment, according to the Rathus Assertiveness Schedule (RAS), were that the assertive-training subjects reported significantly[2] greater gains in acquiring assertive behavior than did control subjects and insignificantly[3] greater gains than did subjects in the discussion group. No significant difference was found between control and discussion subjects. Subjects receiving assertive training also tended to show more assertive behavior than did the other subjects and reported significantly greater reduction of fear in general and of fear associated with social situations in particular.

---

*From "An Experimental Investigation of Assertive Training in a Group Setting," by S. A. Rathus, *Journal of Behavior Therapy and Experimental Psychiatry*, 1972, 3, 81–86. Copyright 1972 by Pergamon Press Ltd. Reprinted by permission.

[2]The word *significant* (and its derivatives), when referring to experimental findings, is used throughout this book in the statistical sense of "statistically significant finding" rather than in the more common sense of "important" or "meaningful."

[3]See note 2 above.

Developing Nonverbal Skills

Serber (1972) notes that most published reports about assertive training deal with developing appropriate verbal behavior but that a most important aspect of assertive behavior—the "paralinguistic component" (how the verbal behavior is expressed, as opposed to just its content) has not received enough attention. The components of nonverbal behavior that he believes are most likely to significantly contribute to "total socially meaningful behavior" are (1) loudness of voice, (2) fluency of spoken words, (3) eye contact, (4) facial expression, (5) body expression, and (6) distance from person with whom one is interacting.

Serber emphasizes that all of these components can be satisfactorily assessed by an experienced clinician or behavioral rater. He says that the most favorable conditions for shaping nonverbal behavior are (1) a clearly defined situation, (2) concentration upon a limited number of nonverbal variables, (3) audiovisual feedback. Serber notes that it is important to work with a situation that can be easily reenacted several times. The individual is encouraged to respond assertively to the situation, and, as he does so, his behavior is videotaped. The most deficient behavior exhibited by the subject is selected for modification, and the individual receives audiovisual feedback with emphasis on this deficient behavior. Appropriate behavior is modeled (practiced by someone) for him, and then the individual practices the behavior himself. Reinforcement follows the practice sessions as the individual's behavior shows improvement (becomes more assertive).

After this brief discussion of some of the literature relevant to our topic, let's explore in depth the behavioral procedures most commonly used in therapist-directed training.

Behavioral Rehearsal and Role Playing

Behavioral rehearsal and role playing are two of the most effective procedures for the development of assertive behavior.

Behavioral rehearsal, as its name indicates, is a rehearsal of behavior; before actually engaging in something, the individual rehearses what he is going to do. This is an age-old practice, which only recently has been recognized as an effective behavior-therapy technique. Just about everyone has thought out loud what he or she was going to say or do at some forthcoming time. When a man tells his wife just how he is going to go up to his boss and ask for a raise, he is carrying out behavioral rehearsal. Refined and adapted to its specific goals, behavioral rehearsal has become perhaps the most frequently used technique in assertive training.

This is Wolpe's (1973) description of behavior rehearsal:

It consists of the acting out of short exchanges between the therapist and the patient in settings from the patient's life. The patient represents himself, and the therapist someone towards whom the patient is unadaptively anxious and inhibited. The therapist starts with a remark, usually oppositional, that the other person might make, and the patient responds as if the situation were "real." His initial response will usually be variously hesitant, defensive, and timid. The therapist then suggests a more appropriate response; and the exchange is run again, revised. The sequence may be repeated again and again until the therapist is satisfied that the patient's utterances have been suitably reshaped. It is necessary to take into account not only the words the patient uses, but also the loudness, firmness, and emotional expressiveness of his voice, and the appropriateness of accompanying bodily movements. The aim of such modeling, shaping, and rehearsing is frequently an effective preparation for the patient to deal with his real "adversary" so that the anxiety the latter evokes may be reciprocally inhibited, and the motor assertive habit established [p. 91].*

Lazarus (1966) defines behavior rehearsal as

a specific procedure which aims to replace deficient or inadequate social or interpersonal responses by efficient and effective behaviour patterns. The patient achieves this by practicing the desired forms of behaviour under the direction and supervision of the therapist [p. 209].

Repeated rehearsals, according to Lazarus, usually diminish the individual's anxieties, so that eventually he is able to respond assertively. Lazarus then provides the following account of a characteristic assertive-training approach using behavioral rehearsal.

In this method patient and therapist role-played various scenes which posed assertive problems for the patient . . . expressing disagreement with a friend's social arrangements, asking a favour, upbraiding a subordinate at work, contradicting a fellow employee, refusing to accede to an unreasonable request, complaining to his employer about the inferior office fixtures, requesting an increment in salary, criticizing his father's attire, questioning his father's values, and so forth. Commencing with the less-demanding situations, each scene was systematically rehearsed until the most troublesome encounters had been enacted to the satisfaction of patient and therapist. The therapist usually role-played the significant persons in the patient's life according to descriptions provided by the latter. The patient's behaviour was shaped by means of constructive criticism as well as modeling procedures in which the therapist assumed the patient's role and demonstrated the desirable response. A situation was regarded as "satisfactorily covered" (1) when the patient was able to enact it without feeling anxious (if he became tense or anxious while rehearsing a scene, deep relaxation was applied until he felt calm again); (2) when his general demeanor, posture, facial expression, inflection in tone, and the like lent substance to his words (repeated play-backs from a tape recorder helped to remove a querulous pitch from his voice); and (3) when agreement was reached that his words and actions would seem fair and fitting to an objective onlooker. In order to expedite the transfer from consulting room to actual life, the patient

*From *The Practice of Behavior Therapy*, by J. Wolpe. Copyright 1973 by Pergamon Press, Inc. Reprinted by permission.

was initially encouraged to apply his newly acquired assertive skills only when negative consequences were highly improbable . . . He soon grew proficient at handling most situations that called for uninhibited and forthright behaviour [Lazarus, 1966, pp. 209–210].*

Behavioral rehearsal is designed to develop or modify specific overt behaviors. In assertive training, this technique is employed to make the overt behaviors in question more assertive. First of all, the specific nature of the individual's nonassertiveness is established. Then, certain desirable behaviors are identified, and the individual rehearses them. By rehearsing these behaviors, the subject finds it easier to later actually implement them.

Role playing is very similar to behavioral rehearsal, since both techniques involve the individual "acting out" some responses. The difference is that behavior rehearsal usually deals with a particular problem situation unique to the individual and causing him great anxiety; role playing, instead, deals with more general situations—situations not unique to the individual, in other words. The person plays the role of another (generally that of someone with whom he interacts frequently, such as his spouse or his supervisor), with the therapist playing the role of the individual in training.

The goal of role playing is to permit the person to practice behavior that otherwise he would inhibit and to give him an opportunity to see the situation from the point of view of the other person and, consequently, to gain additional perspective regarding his own behavior.

McFall and Marston (1970), in noting the paucity of systematic research on the subject, stated that behavioral rehearsal, as generally described, is a rather vague amalgamation of various techniques and procedures. They said:

> . . . the behavior rehearsal treatment procedure, as typically described, appears to be complex, unsystematic, and unstandardized, relative to other behavior therapy techniques [p. 295].

Using what they called a "constructive" approach,[4] McFall and Marston carried out several investigations to determine the relative effectiveness of various procedures used in behavioral rehearsal to develop assertive behavior. Specifically, they studied (1) whether response rehearsal (rehearsing assertive responses to situations calling for them) leads to a significant improvement in assertive behavior, and (2) whether the addition of performance feedback via the playback of tape-recorded responses significantly adds to the results obtained by rehearsal alone. For their studies, McFall and Marston developed a standardized, semiautomated procedure in which the responses of nonassertive subjects to a series of role-played situations calling for assertive behavior were audiotaped. The subjects received four sessions of practice, in which

*From "Behavior Rehearsal vs. Non-Directive Therapy vs. Advice in Effecting Behaviour Change," by A. A. Lazarus, *Behaviour Research and Therapy*, 1966, 4, 209–212. Reprinted by permission of Pergamon Press Ltd.

[4]For a description of this kind of research strategy, see McFall and Marston, 1970, p. 302.

they were to respond assertively to the role-played situations. The subjects were assigned to one of the following four groups: (1) behavior rehearsal with performance feedback, (2) behavior rehearsal without performance feedback, (3) placebo therapy (measuring, among other things, the nontreatment effects of attention and suggestion), and (4) control.

At the end of the procedure, the subjects' responses recorded before and after treatment were compared, and the participants rated themselves on two 5-point scales measuring (1) the degree of anxiety they experienced and (2) how well they felt they had performed. The recorded responses were also evaluated by outside judges who didn't know whether the recording they were listening to had been made before or after treatment. Analysis of the results showed that groups 1 and 2 (rehearsal with feedback and rehearsal without feedback) had developed significantly more assertive behavior than either group 3 or 4. No significant difference was found between group 1 and group 2 (the two rehearsal groups), although group 1, because of the feedback received, showed a slight increase in assertiveness.

Modeling

Modeling is a technique similar to behavioral rehearsal and role playing. It consists in watching someone (the model) enact some particular behavior that, because of anxiety or other inhibiting factors, the person has difficulty engaging in. In other words by observing someone else perform an assertive act, the individual learns to overcome his anxieties and inhibitions connected with that behavior and to engage in the behavior himself. To achieve the desired effects, this technique generally requires several sessions (up to 20) over a period of time.

Bandura (1971a) states that modeling is governed by four interrelated processes: (1) *attentional processes*, which refer to the individual attending to what he is observing, and which entail not only being attentive but also being able to recognize and differentiate the model's behavior; (2) *retention processes*, by which the observer retains the original observations in some symbolic form, either imaginal or verbal; (3) *motoric reproduction processes*, which involve using these symbolic representations to guide one's own performance; and (4) *reinforcement and motivational processes*, which refer to the consequences of observing modeled behavior. Modeling can be used to effect change in three broad and important areas of psychological functioning: (1) to transmit new patterns of behavior, (2) to eliminate unwarranted fears and inhibitions, and (3) to facilitate expression of preexisting modes of response.

Modeling can be used very effectively and in a variety of ways in assertive training. This is how Bandura (1971b) describes an effective modeling approach:

First, desired behavior is repeatedly modeled, preferably by multiple models who demonstrate progressively more difficult performances. Second, observers are provided with necessary guidance and ample opportunities to enact the modeled behaviors at each step in the graduated sequence of activities under favorable conditions. The latter procedures are ideally suited for inducing psychological changes, but they are unlikely to endure unless established behaviors produce rewarding consequences. Arrangement of favorable reinforcement contingencies to maintain matching behavior, therefore, constitutes the third component in the powerful compound method [p. 703].

Thus, in modeling, the individual deficient in assertive skills watches several models—some of them similar in age and background to the individual—perform assertive behaviors, either in the flesh or on video tape. The tasks being modeled are increasingly assertive, and each one is followed by reinforcing consequences. For example, the model is shown demanding that improperly done work be redone correctly; this request is followed by the prompt, nonhostile compliance of the person to whom the model's request was addressed. After observing the model, the individual in training translates what he has observed into action by carrying out the behavior himself. It is of vital importance that this implementation of the modeled behavior be done on a gradual basis and that reinforcing consequences follow each attempt.

Eisler, Hersen, and Miller (1973) investigated the effects of modeling on components of assertive behavior. Thirty male hospitalized psychiatric patients, who were deemed to be in need of assertive training, were assigned to one of the three following groups, with ten subjects in each group: (1) modeling, (2) practice-control, and (3) test-retest control. The subjects were instructed to respond to a series of five interpersonal interactions calling for assertive behavior, and their responses were videotaped before and after treatment. Subjects in the modeling group were exposed to four sessions of a videotaped model who responded assertively to the five situations. After each modeling session, the subjects were instructed to respond to each of the five situations. Subjects in the practice-control group were instructed to respond to each of the five situations, without being exposed to the videotapes. The test-retest control subjects simply responded to the videotaped scenes.

The pre- and posttreatment videotaped responses of all subjects to the five interpersonal situations were rated on the basis of the following eight components of behavior: (1) duration of looking, (2) duration of reply, (3) latency of response, (4) loudness of voice, (5) compliance content, (6) content requesting new behavior, (7) assertive affect, and (8) overall assertiveness.

The videotapes of all subjects were then evaluated by judges who did not know what treatment group the subjects belonged to. Analysis of the results indicated that those subjects assigned to the modeling group behaved significantly more assertively than those in either the practice-control or the test-retest groups.

Practice, Instructions, and Modeling

In a related study, Hersen, Eisler, Miller, Johnson, and Pinkston (1973) investigated the effects of practice, instructions, and modeling on assertive behavior. Nonassertive subjects were assigned to one of the five following situations: (1) test-retest, (2) practice-control, (3) instructions, (4) modeling, and (5) modeling plus instructions. All subjects received the same instructions and then were videotaped while responding to two situations calling for assertive responses. These responses served as a pretreatment measurement. The test-retest subjects did nothing further until the experiment was over, at which time they responded again to the same situations, and their responses were again videotaped. Practice-control subjects were told that they had performed satisfactorily but were encouraged to try and do better on a subsequent trial. Subjects in the instructions group were given the following detailed instructions:

> That was o.k., but try and do better next time. Make sure you talk long enough so that Mrs. Pinkston [model] understands what you mean. Look at her when you talk. Tell her how you want things changed to make the situation better. Tell her what you expect her to do. Also, make sure you talk loudly enough. Let me repeat what I want you to do. Make sure that you talk long enough so that Mrs. Pinkston understands what you mean. Look at her when you talk. Tell her how you want things changed to make the situation better. Also, make sure you talk loudly enough [Hersen et al., 1973, p. 447].

Subjects in the modeling group received the following instructions after the pretest described above and before each practice session: "That was o.k., but try and do better this time. Watch our model on the videotape playback. This may help you express yourself better" (p. 447). Those in the modeling-plus-instructions group received modeling alone and instructions alone after the pretest and before each treatment session.

The results of the experiment indicated that observation of a videotaped model, along with focused instructions, facilitated the development of assertive responses to specific situations. The results also showed that, although the modeling-plus-instructions group was superior or at least equal to both the modeling-alone and the instructions-alone groups on five of seven indices of assertiveness, each of the latter two groups effected the greatest change in one of the two measurements. Hersen et al. (1973) made the following very interesting comment, based on their study and related research:

> These data point to the differential effects of these specific techniques on the particular verbal and non-verbal components of assertiveness. In consideration of the actual clinical situation, it would appear that each non-verbal and verbal component should be given individual attention (Eisler, Miller, Hersen, 1973; Eisler, Hersen, & Miller, 1973; Serber, 1972) throughout the full course of assertive training. The use of the video-medium is ideally suited for this purpose [p. 450].

Behavioral Rehearsal with Modeling and Coaching

Another constructive contribution to the investigation of the use of behavioral rehearsal in developing assertive behavior was offered by McFall and Lillesand (1971) in a study of the effects of symbolic modeling and therapist-coached rehearsal in conjunction with the feedback procedure reported by McFall and Marston (1970). Thirty-three college students who rated themselves as deficient in the ability to refuse unreasonable requests were randomly assigned to one of three groups: (1) overt rehearsal with modeling and coaching; (2) covert rehearsal[5] with modeling and coaching; and (3) control. All subjects were seen individually for two sessions, one week apart. Prior to treatment, all subjects were administered a behavioral role-playing test in which they were instructed to respond aloud to each of nine prerecorded situations calling for assertive behavior. An example of such a situation is presented below.

> *Narrator:* A person you do not know very well is going home for the weekend. He, or she, has some books which are due at the library and asks if you would take them back, so they won't be overdue. From where you live it is a twenty-five minute walk to the library, the books are heavy, and you hadn't planned on going near the library that weekend. What do you say? [McFall & Lillesand, 1971, p. 315].

All the subjects responded aloud to the situation. For the control subjects this concluded the first session, and they were dismissed. Treatment for the two remaining groups was identical except that (1) the overt-rehearsal subjects were instructed to rehearse aloud, while the covert-rehearsal subjects were instructed to imagine responding, and (2) the overt subjects heard a recorded replay of their practice behavior, while the covert subjects spent the same period of time simply "reflecting" on their response. The refusal (assertive response) training for each of the situations was as follows:

> (a) The narrator described the situation; (b) S responded overtly or covertly; (c) S heard the responses of one male and one female assertive model; (d) the narrator coached S regarding what makes a good assertive response in the situation; (e) S either heard his response replayed or reflected on it; (f) the situation was repeated; and S responded overtly or covertly again [McFall & Lillesand, 1971, p. 315].

The following is a segment of a training tape that further illustrates the procedures used by McFall and Lillesand.

> *Narrator:* A person in one of your classes—someone whom you do not know very well—borrowed your class notes weeks ago, then failed to return them at

---

[5]Covert rehearsal refers to the use of one's imagination to visualize the response one would make to a certain situation. For a detailed discussion of covert techniques, see pp. 77–80.

the next class, thus forcing you to take notes on scrap paper. Now this person comes up to you again and says, "Hey, mind if I borrow your class notes again?" What do you say? (Subject practices responding either overtly or covertly.)

Narrator: Now, listen to the responses of two assertive subjects to this same situation.

Male Model: You didn't return my notes last time, so I'm not going to lend them to you this time.

Female Model: No, I just can't be sure you're going to have them back in time.

Narrator (coaching): Notice that both of these assertive subjects let the person know that their refusal was based on his past behavior. Their responses were brief and without any ambiguity. Their voices expressed some irritation over the past behavior of this person, but in general their responses were well controlled. Now (listen to/think back to) your response to this situation and compare it to the responses of the models you have just heard. (Playback or 10-second pause.)

Narrator: Now, you will hear the same situation again. This time try to make your response more assertive. (Repeat situation. Subject practices responding.) [pp. 315–316].*

Analysis of the results, based on self-reports, behavioral laboratory measures, and video follow-up measures attests to the therapeutic efficacy of behavioral rehearsal. Subjects treated with the rehearsal therapy with modeling and coaching improved dramatically in terms of assertive-refusal behavior when compared with the control subjects. The results also show that the covert-rehearsal subjects improved as much if not more than the overt-rehearsal subjects.

Rehearsal, Modeling, and Coaching

McFall and Twentyman (1973) reported on four experiments dealing with the contributions of rehearsal, modeling, and coaching to assertive training.

Study One

This first study dealt with systematically dismantling the McFall and Lillesand (1971) treatment procedure and assessing any overall decrease in treatment results. Subjects deficient in assertive-refusal behavior were randomly assigned to one of these six treatment groups: (1) rehearsal, modeling,

---

*From "Behavior Rehearsal with Modeling and Coaching in Assertion Training," by R. M. McFall and D. B. Lillesand, *Journal of Abnormal Psychology,* 1971, 77, 313–323. Copyright 1971 by the American Psychological Association. Reprinted by permission.

and coaching; (2) rehearsal and modeling; (3) rehearsal and coaching; (4) rehearsal only; (5) modeling and coaching; and (6) control. All subjects were seen individually for two 45-minute experimental sessions, one week apart. A behavioral role-playing test was administered to all subjects, and their responses were recorded. The treatment procedure was similar to that outlined in the McFall and Lillesand (1971) study. Modeling was presented on audio tape, with coaching administered live by an assistant (someone who was not a therapist). The results showed that a behavioral program consisting of rehearsal and coaching can significantly improve assertive-refusal behavior in nonassertive subjects. The results further indicated that the effects of the rehearsal and coaching components were independent and additive. Audio modeling was found to add little or nothing to the results obtained by rehearsal or rehearsal plus coaching.

Study Two

This study investigated the improvements in assertive behavior associated with covert rehearsal, modeling, and coaching, respectively. Nonassertive subjects were randomly assigned to one of the following three groups: (1) covert rehearsal, modeling, and coaching; (2) covert rehearsal, and coaching; and (3) covert rehearsal only. The experimental procedure was similar to that of Study One. The rehearsal-alone group was regarded as a minimal-treatment group, against which the results of the other two groups were compared. The results, according to McFall and Twentyman (1973),

> provided corroborative evidence that the assertion-training program consisting of rehearsal and coaching produced positive treatment effects, but that the modeling component, when combined with the rehearsal and coaching components, added little if any to the treatment effects [p. 208].

They further found that treatment effects generalized from trained to untrained refusal situations.

Study Three

Study Three was conducted to shed further light on the role of modeling in the development of assertive behavior. Several questions raised in analyzing the results of the two previous studies dealt with the models' behavior—that is, whether the models were too competent, too extreme, or somehow too unrealistic to elicit emulation. To investigate this problem, Study Three utilized the same basic research design used in the other two studies, except that one-half of the subjects listened to the same models used in the previous studies, while the other half listened to a new set of models, whose responses were "more tactful, more hesitant, and less extreme." The results indicated that the failure of the modeling component to add anything significant in terms of increasing assertiveness to what had been obtained by rehearsal and coaching "probably was not a function of the particular characteristics of the models employed" (McFall & Twentyman, 1973, p. 210). The results further indicated no difference between overt and covert rehearsal when the playback component was eliminated.

Study Four

In a continued attempt to investigate the contribution modeling can make to the development of assertive behavior, Study Four compared audiotaped modeling with audio-videotaped modeling. The research design was basically the same used in previous studies, but, unlike the other investigations, Study Four compared the results obtained from audio feedback with those obtained from audiovisual feedback. A professional television studio was employed to prepare a videotaped adaptation of the material presented on the previous audiotape. Special care was taken in making the videotape to assure that the accompanying sound track could easily be used by itself. Treatment consisted of two sessions of 40 minutes each, dealing with refusal behavior.

The results of this study demonstrated that "the addition of a visual component to the assertion-training program failed to enhance treatment effects in any detectable way" (McFall & Twentyman, 1973, p. 213).

In discussing the results of their four experiments, McFall and Twentyman stated that behavioral rehearsal and coaching were responsible for the significant improvement observed both on self-report and on behavioral laboratory measures. Here are some of the important conclusions the investigators drew in regard to rehearsal.

> Response rehearsal, along with the feedback it produces, appears to be the mechanism by which newly acquired responses are strengthened, refined, and integrated into the repertoire. In the present research, overt rehearsal, covert rehearsal, and a combination of the two were found to be equally effective modes of practice. In general, however, the effectiveness of a particular rehearsal procedure probably depends on the particular response skill being trained [p. 215].

As to coaching, McFall and Twentyman (1973) took issue with Bandura's (1971a) suggestion that coaching is merely a special form of modeling. They stated: "There is no more justification for regarding instructions as 'verbal modeling' than for regarding observational modeling merely as 'visual instructions' " (p. 215). McFall and Twentyman then proceeded to clarify the distinction between modeling and instructions in terms of the types of information they provide.

> Modeling provides subjects with examples of specific behaviors from which general principles must be abstracted; instructional coaching, on the other hand, provides subjects with general conceptual principles for which specific behavioral referents must be generated. Whereas modeling procedures tend to function independently, coaching procedures tend to function deductively [p. 215].

Although they noted that the efficacy of modeling in terms of developing assertive behavior had not been demonstrated in their four experiments, they did raise two questions: (1) What role would reinforcing consequences of the modeled behavior have? (2) What effect would modeling alone have in comparison to no treatment at all?

Covert Conditioning Techniques

These techniques refer in assertive training to the use of one's imagination to visualize various behaviors. The imagined behavior may be followed by visualized rewarding consequences (covert reinforcement) or visualized aversive consequences (covert sensitization). Covert modeling, in which the individual imagines others engaging in certain behaviors, which are then followed by either positive or negative consequences, is also used as a covert conditioning technique.

Covert Reinforcement

The individual utilizing covert reinforcement is instructed to visualize carrying out a specified assertive behavior. After imagining carrying out this assertive behavior, he is instructed to imagine very rewarding and pleasing consequences of the behavior. For example, the individual may be instructed to imagine successfully asserting himself to a fellow worker (a particularly difficult task for him) and then to imagine his fellow worker and some bystanders applauding his assertiveness. The basic idea is to increase the incidence of assertiveness by following assertive imagery with positive-reinforcing imagery.

The use of covert reinforcement can be very helpful in assertive training, because it can break the vicious chain of thinking about the possible unpleasant consequences of assertive behavior. Typically, individuals who have difficulty asserting tend to be in an approach-avoidance situation. They want to assert themselves but are afraid because they are thinking of the unpleasant consequences that may follow their assertion. Their habit of thinking of negative consequences serves to maintain their high levels of anxiety in regard to assertion; therefore, what they need to do is to replace the response pattern of thinking negative consequences with that of thinking positive-reinforcing consequences.

Covert Sensitization

Covert sensitization is a technique that may be of value in eliminating nonassertive and aggressive behavior (in contrast to covert reinforcement, which is used to develop assertive behavior). In covert sensitization, the individual is instructed to visualize a typical situation in which he is behaving in an unadaptive manner and then to visualize, as vividly as possible, extremely aversive consequences of his behavior. The therapist describes the scene, paying particular attention to all kinds of noxious details. These aversive consequences may consist of ridicule, ostracism, verbal counterattack—whatever is particularly aversive to the particular individual. The visualized aversive consequences of a certain behavior are supposed to help the individual eliminate that behavior. It should be noted, however, that the findings reported by the literature on covert sensitization to date are inconclusive (Thoresen & Mahoney, 1974).

Covert Modeling

Kazdin (1974) investigated the effects of covert modeling (imagining a person performing assertive behavior) and covert modeling plus reinforcement (again, imagining a model performing assertive behavior, but with reinforcing consequences following model's behavior). The assessment of the effects of these two techniques involved the use of subjects' self-report measurement of their ability to assert themselves, refuse others, and cope with anxiety-provoking situations, as well as a behavioral role-playing test in which the subjects were instructed to respond to recorded situations calling for assertive behavior. The 45 subjects were randomly assigned to four groups: covert modeling, covert modeling plus reinforcement, and two control groups, one (no-model controls) designed to control the effects of just imagining assertion-relevant scenes and the other (delayed-treatment subjects) designed to control the influence of repeated assessment in the absence of any treatment. Stimulus material consisted of 35 scenes that the subjects were to imagine during treatment. Five scenes were used in the first session, and ten in each session thereafter. All of the scenes consisted of these three parts: (1) a description of the context and situation calling for assertive behavior, (2) a model engaging in assertive behavior, and (3) rewarding consequences following the model's behavior.

Treatment was carried out individually over a two-week period. Covert-modeling-plus-reinforcement subjects were instructed to imagine scenes including all three parts (the situation calling for assertive behavior, the model's assertive response, and the rewarding consequences). Covert-modeling subjects were instructed to imagine scenes consisting of the situation calling for an assertive response and the model actually making the assertive response. No-model controls were simply instructed to imagine the situation calling for an assertive response. They were not instructed to imagine assertive behavior on the part of the model or to imagine that reinforcing consequences would follow. The delayed-treatment subjects participated in the pre- and posttreatment assessment only. Treatment was then offered to them.

The results indicated that covert modeling can effectively increase assertive behavior. Some subjects in the model and model-reinforcement groups achieved significantly more assertive behavior than either of the control groups. Model reinforcement achieved slightly more assertive behavior than model alone, but the difference was not significant.

Kazdin (1975) further investigated the development of assertive behavior by the use of covert modeling. He studied two variables—the number of models and the consequences of the modeled behavior—and took into consideration the additional factor of assessing imagery. This relates to the fact that, when subjects are instructed to imagine certain material, it is difficult to determine whether they actually imagine the specified material. Kazdin's subjects were instructed to recreate in their minds a scene they had just watched and, as they were doing so, to describe the scene they were imagining. These descriptions were tape-recorded and compared with the original material. In the treatment phase of this study, 24 female and 30 male subjects were randomly assigned to one of the following five groups, and treatment was administered in four sessions over a two-week period: (1) single model, with reinforcement (imagining always the same person, similar to oneself, modeling assertive behavior, with favorable consequences following assertive performance); (2) single model, no reinforcement (imagining always the same model, similar to oneself, engaging in assertive behavior, but with no favorable consequences); (3) multiple models, with reinforcement (imagining a different model in each treatment session, with favorable consequences following the imagined performance); (4) multiple model, with no reinforcement (imagining a different person in each session, but with no favorable consequences); and (5) nonassertive-model control (simply imagining a model whose performance does not involve making an assertive response).

The results of the experiment, according to Kazdin (1975), were the following:

a. Imagining several models engaging in assertive performance led to greater changes in assertive behavior than did imagining a single model.

b. Imagining favorable consequences following model performance enhanced modeling effects.

c. Imagining assertion-relevant scenes without an assertive model was not as consistently associated with changes in assertive behavior as were covert modeling conditions.

d. The gains effected with covert modeling transferred to novel role-playing situations and tended to be maintained up to four months of follow-up on a self-report measure.

e. The within-session reports of imagery were useful in determining the extent to which subjects adhered to the imagery conditions to which they were assigned and in revealing divergence from the scenes presented [p. 723].*

*From "Covert Modeling, Imagery Assessment, and Assertive Behavior," by A. E. Kazdin, *Journal of Consulting and Clinical Psychology*, 1975, 43(5), 716–724. Copyright 1975 by American Psychological Association. Reprinted by permission.

In terms of assessing imagery—that is, checking if the subjects' imageries were faithful to the scenes presented—the differences among the groups were minor. The subjects in the model-reinforcement group added more descriptive material to the scenes than the subjects in the nonreinforcement group.

The Use of Reinforcement

Reinforcement, as we have seen in Chapter Two, is a behavioral consequence that strengthens behavior by being added to the situation (positive reinforcer) or withdrawn from the situation (negative reinforcer). We have also seen that, since behavior is controlled by its consequences, most of our responses are strengthened, maintained, or weakened by the events that follow their occurrence. Assertive training capitalizes on this principle by reinforcing assertive responses in order to strengthen or maintain assertive behavior.

Reinforcement in assertive training may be administered in a variety of ways. According to Wolpe (1969), "the motor act itself is reinforced by its consequences, such as the attainment of control of a social situation, reduction in anxiety, and, later, the approbation of the therapist" (p. 62). *Self-reinforcement* refers to the individual applying his own reinforcement. This may be as simple as his telling himself "Congratulations! You handled that situation well," when he effectively asserts himself to someone. It may involve, instead, some tangible self-reward, such as indulging in something particularly pleasant in return for carrying out desired assertiveness. The important point is that in self-reinforcement the individual himself rewards his own behavior.

Funny as it may seem, literally patting one's own back is a good way of reinforcing expressions of assertive behavior. Obviously, you can't do that everywhere and at all times. But, if you can manage a little privacy, go ahead and pat yourself on your back, telling yourself that you handled the situation well. You will be surprised how effective a reinforcement that (apparently silly) little pat on your own back is, particularly if, at the same time, you tell yourself "Good job! Very good! You handled that situation very well. Congratulations!"

Karoly and Kanfer (1974) see self-reinforcement as a component of the three-phased process of self regulation, which consists in (1) self-monitoring, (2) self-evaluation, and (3) self-reinforcement. According to this view, the application of self-reinforcement (or self-punishment) follows the determination of how one's current performance relates to a subjectively held standard—that is, how we feel we should have behaved. Self-reward is supposed to follow when one's behavior equals or exceeds this standard, and, conversely, self-punishment is supposed to be a consequence of the individual perceiving his or her behavior as a substandard performance.

Thoresen and Mahoney (1974) have summarized as follows some basic generalizations that seem warranted by existing research on self-reinforcement, particularly as affected by modeling:

1. Self-rewarding behaviors may be established through exposure to models.
2. Self-imposed standards of reinforcement are affected by previous modeling experiences.
3. Discrepancies between the competencies of a model and a subject may attenuate the extent to which modeled standards are adopted.
4. Discrepancies between a model's self-imposed reward criteria and those that he imposes on a subject dramatically weaken the latter's subsequent adherence to even lenient self-reward standards. One possible exception to this generalization is that in which the discrepancy favors the subject.
5. Consistency between models enhances adoption of self-reward standards.
6. The effects of socially learned self-reward patterns are basically equivalent to those of externally administered reinforcement systems in maintaining effortful responding.
7. When given the opportunity to choose or alter their own self-reward standard, subjects will often impose very high work requirements on themselves [p. 78].*

Related to self-reinforcement is *therapist-administered reinforcement.* Hersen, Eisler, and Miller (1973), after reviewing the clinical literature on the subject, stated that therapist's reinforcement of assertive verbalizations occurs in the course of typical assertive training. This reinforcement is primarily verbal in nature but may also be nonverbal. As the individual undergoing assertive training relates his or her experiences in the therapy sessions, the alert therapist gives verbal as well as nonverbal (smiling, nodding, and so on) reinforcement every time the patient reports assertive behavior. Verbal reinforcement by the therapist may consist of simply making such comments as "That's good, Sal, you really asserted yourself well."

In the early stages of assertive training, the therapist may enlist the aid of significant others to further reinforce assertive behavior. By "significant others" we mean the individual's spouse, parents, children, siblings, and close friends and relatives. These significant others are encouraged to verbally reinforce every instance of assertive behavior and, conversely, not to reinforce nonassertive behavior.

As assertive training continues and the individual becomes more proficient at asserting himself, reinforcement will come from others in the form of the attention and respect the individual's assertive behavior commands; it will also be self-generated in the form of greater self-confidence. At this point, these kinds of reinforcement are sufficient to maintain the individual's assertive behavior.

---

*From *Behavioral Self-Control*, by C. E. Thoresen and M. J. Mahoney. Copyright 1974 by Holt, Rinehart and Winston. Reprinted by permission.

An Example of the Use of Reinforcement in Assertive Training

MacPherson (1972) reported on the selective reinforcement and extinction of nonassertive and aggressive behavior. The subject was a 45-year-old woman, who was hypercritical and aggressive toward her husband and, at the same time, dominated by her mother, who lived with them. Role playing was used to help the woman develop more adaptive behavior. The therapist described certain situations, and the patient first responded to them as she normally would. Then the situations were presented again, and the woman responded in a manner that she and the therapist had agreed to be assertive. The following are a few of the 20 situations developed in the course of therapy. The perceptive reader will notice that some of these examples of assertive behavior are quite strong; under certain circumstances, they would clearly be examples of aggressive, rather than assertive, behavior. This study is presented here because it provides a useful illustration of aggressive behavior being replaced with assertive behavior.

Your mother says to you "Your husband should help you more instead of going off . . ."
Nonassertive Response (NA): "Yes, I suppose you're right, he should."
Assertive Response (A): "That's a matter between me and my husband, it's nothing to do with you" [p. 100].

Another situation dealing with the domineering mother is the following:

You are shopping with your mother and she says "I wouldn't get that, it's a stupid waste of money."
NA: Do you really think so? Well, in that case I won't get it."
A: "It's my money, and I will spend it how I wish" [p. 100].

Here are two situations dealing with the husband:

Your husband comes in late, and the supper you have made is spoiled.
Aggressive (A): "Where the hell have you been? The supper is ruined."
Nonaggressive (NA): "I'm sorry your supper is a bit dried up. Shall I get you something else?"

Your husband comes home after working in the office and falls asleep in the chair. When he wakes up you say:
A: "For goodness sake, try to keep awake so that we can both watch television."
NA: "You must be very tired. Can I get you something?" [p. 100].*

---

*From "Selective Operant Conditioning and Deconditioning of Assertive Modes of Behavior," by E. L. MacPherson, *Journal of Behavior Therapy and Experimental Psychiatry,* 1972, 3(2), 99–102.

Information Giving, Coaching, and Homework

Much of what goes on in traditional psychotherapy involves the exchange of information between the individual and the therapist—both giving *and* receiving information. Along with the exchange of information, therapy may also make use of coaching and homework. Coaching refers to the therapist giving advice to the individual, with the expectation that he will benefit from it. Homework consists in specific tasks that the individual is expected to carry out on his own.

These techniques are also used very effectively in assertive training. Hersen, Eisler, and Miller (1973) say:

> The specific techniques contributing to the overall success of assertive training have been examined in analogue designs (Eisler et al., 1973; Friedman, 1971; Hersen et al., 1973; McFall and Marston, 1970; McFall and Lillesand, 1971). Although a full understanding of all elements producing change has not been achieved, some definite patterns are beginning to emerge. Most striking is the extent to which an active process takes place between the therapist and his patient. Indeed, the relationship approximates that of teacher and student. The therapist instructs, models, coaches, and reinforces appropriate verbal and nonverbal responses. Concurrently, the patient first practices his newly developed repertoire in the consulting room and then in actual situations requiring assertive responses [p. 518].

Simply by talking with the individual, the therapist can become aware of many misconceptions and inappropriate behaviors on the part of the individual and work with him to correct them. This interchange between therapist and individual continues throughout therapy. Many small, specific problems may be handled by subtle alterations in the individual's behavior— alterations that may be brought about by advice, suggestion, and coaching followed by appropriate homework. For example, advice and coaching on how to ask for a date may be followed by graduated homework assignments of (1) making it a point to say hello to three different girls in one day; (2) striking up a conversation with one girl on another day; (3) striking up another conversation with that same girl on another day; and finally (4) asking her for a date.

Use of Video- and Audiotapes

The use of video- and/or audiotape recording can be of value in assertive training, because it permits the individual to see or hear himself the way others see and hear him. The person is instructed to interact with a group of people in his normal manner; as he does so, he is being recorded. By viewing the videotape or listening to the audiotape playback, the person can see and/ or hear the instances of his nonassertiveness or aggressiveness. Videotape provides, of course, more complete information; but even audiotape alone is useful.

Video or audio feedback is seldom used by itself; rather, it is used in conjunction with some of the techniques discussed earlier. It is particularly effective in behavioral rehearsal and modeling; the individual rehearses assertive behaviors and then receives feedback about these behaviors.

The work of numerous researchers (Eisler, Hersen, & Miller, 1973; Friedman, 1971; Hersen, Eisler, & Miller, 1973; McFall & Lillesand, 1971; McFall & Marston, 1970) indicates that the use of videotape and/or audiotape is helpful in the development of assertive behavior. Serber (1972) lists audiovisual feedback as one of the three most useful means for developing nonverbal assertive behavior.

Videotape can be used in assessing pre- and posttreatment behavior, with independent judges rating the behavior in terms of verbal and nonverbal assertiveness. The Behavioral Assertiveness Test (Eisler, Miller, & Hersen, 1973) is based on a series of 14 interpersonal situations calling for assertive behavior. A female model is used in a variety of test situations, playing such roles as wife, sales clerk, and waitress. The subject is instructed to relate as he normally would to the situation presented by a narrator. The model then makes a statement, to which the subject is instructed to reply. His behavior is videotaped as he makes his responses. The behavior of the person is then rated by judges in terms of its assertiveness. Here are several typical situations in the Behavioral Assertiveness Test:

> *Narrator:* You have just come home from work, and as you settle down to read the newspaper you discover that your wife has cut out an important article in order to get a recipe that is on the back of it. You really like to read the whole newspaper.
> *Role Model Wife:* I just wanted to cut out a recipe before I forgot about it.
>
> *Narrator:* You have just punished your son for his inconsiderate behavior and told him that he must stay in his room for the rest of the afternoon. Your wife feels sorry for him and tells him that he can go out to play.
> *Role Model Wife:* It's so nice outside; it's a shame to make him stay in his room.
>
> *Narrator:* You come home late one night, and your wife demands an explanation of why you are so late. As soon as you begin to explain, she interrupts you and starts screaming about how inconsiderate you are.
> *Role Model Wife:* I don't care what happened. You are the most inconsiderate person in the world for making me worry about you.
>
> *Narrator:* You have just bought a new shotgun, the one you've always wanted.
> *Role Model Wife:* You didn't need another shotgun. You have too many now.
> [Eisler, Miller, & Hersen, 1973, p. 296].*

Video- and audiotape can be effectively used in all phases of assertive training—to assess the need for assertive training, to develop assertive behavior, to assess the change in behavior by viewing pre- and posttreatment tape, and to maintain assertive behavior. The use of video feedback in assertive training has been investigated by Galassi, Galassi, and Litz (1974) and by Rathus (1973b). Although additional research is needed to determine the efficacy of video feedback, the present literature indicates that it is of value in assertive training.

Relaxation Training

Many forms of anxiety, fear, anger, and related emotional discomforts are learned behaviors. Their expression in situations calling instead for assertive behavior is also the result of learning and interferes with the development of assertion. Training in deep muscle relaxation can be helpful in the extinction of these unadaptive responses.

The individual troubled by inappropriate emotional reactions and who wants to develop proficiency in muscle relaxation can make use of a variety of exercises and techniques that have been developed for that purpose.

Different people relax in different ways. The term *relaxation* as used in this book refers to the complete absence of any tension in the mind and body. To accomplish this kind of relaxation, specific training and conscious effort are required. We believe that, with time and practice, most people can learn to achieve this kind of relaxation, characterized by a complete lack of tension and by a feeling of calmness and tranquility.

Deep muscle relaxation offers many benefits and is effective in alleviating a wide variety of problems related to emotional disorders (Jacobson, 1938). Chronic anxiety can have harmful effects on the body. For example, when you are anxious, your heart beats faster, your blood pressure increases, and adrenalin is pumped into your blood. These and other physiological reactions are the body's way of preparing to either "fight or run"; your body is mobilized, prepared for immediate action. This mobilization is vital when you encounter danger, since it enables you to draw upon strengths not otherwise available. Unfortunately for them, many people, especially non-assertive and aggressive individuals, walk around fully mobilized much of the time; they are chronically prepared for a fight-or-run situation—a condition generally referred to as anxiety or hypertension.

The individual undergoing assertive training can practice deep relaxation before engaging in a situation in which he will attempt to assert himself. Having gone through the relaxation exercises, he will be in a better position to carry out the assertive responses. Relaxation training also helps to reduce anxiety in general.

Detailed relaxation exercises for use in assertive training are provided in Appendix B.

Positive Assertion and Situational Determinants
of Assertive Behavior

Eisler, Hersen, Miller, and Blanchard (1975) note that most studies on assertive training have dealt with what Wolpe (1969) refers to as "hostile assertiveness" and have failed to consider positive assertion—the expression of positive feelings. These researchers also point to another issue neglected by studies on assertive training—the role of the social-interpersonal context in determining whether a response is assertive. To emphasize the cultural and social relativity of what is considered assertive behavior, they cite as an example someone cutting ahead of you while you are waiting in line to buy theater tickets. What is considered an assertive response on your part will depend, among other things, on the age, sex, and relationship to you of the offending individual. In other words, no behavioral response should be viewed in isolation; rather, it should be studied in the situational context in which it occurs.

Eisler and his colleagues studied some of the behavioral components of negative assertion and systematically examined the effects of social context on interpersonal behavior in assertive situations. Male subjects were exposed to situations calling for an assertive response to a person with whom they had familiarity. An effort was made to delineate in each situation behaviors that would differentiate high- and low-assertive subjects.

The subjects—all males and either married or formerly married—were exposed to 32 role-played situations that called for assertive responses. Of these situations, 16 required the subject to express positive feelings, such as praise, appreciation, and affection, and the other 16 called for the expression of negative feelings, such as anger, displeasure, and disappointment. In half of the scenes the role-playing partner was male and in the other half female. One-half of the situations involved responding to a familiar partner, and one-half to an unfamiliar partner.

Here are some samples of the role-played situations:

Male-Positive-Familiar

Narrator: You have been working on a difficult job all week; your boss comes over with a smile on his face. Your boss says: "That's a very good job you have done; I'm going to give you a raise next week."

Male-Positive-Unfamiliar

Narrator: You are the leader of the company bowling team. Your team is slightly behind, when one of the men on your team makes three strikes in a row to even up the score. You are really proud of him. He says: "How did you like that one?"

Male-Negative-Familiar

Narrator: You have had a very busy day at work and are tired. Your boss comes in and asks you to stay late for the third time this week. You really feel you would like to go home on time tonight. Your boss says: "I'm leaving now; would you mind staying late again tonight and finishing this work for me?"

Male-Negative-Unfamiliar

Narrator: You go to a ballgame with reserved-seat tickets. When you arrive you find that someone has put his coat in the seat for which you have reserved tickets. You ask him to remove his coat, and he tells you that he is saving that seat for a friend. He says: "I'm sorry, this seat is saved."

Female-Positive-Familiar

Narrator: Your wife has just bought a new outfit and is trying it on. You really like it and think that she looks very nice in it. Your wife says: "Well, how do I look in this outfit?"

Female-Positive-Unfamiliar

Narrator: You are in a restaurant, and the waitress has just served you an excellent meal cooked just the way you like it. You are pleased with her prompt, efficient service. She comes by and says: "I hope you enjoyed your dinner, sir."

Female-Negative-Familiar

Narrator: You are in the middle of watching an exciting football game on television. Your wife walks in and changes the channel, as she does every time you are watching a good game. Your wife says: "Let's watch the movie instead; it's really supposed to be good."

Female-Negative-Unfamiliar

Narrator: You are in a crowded grocery store and are in a hurry because you are already late for an appointment. You pick up one small item and get in line to pay for it. Then a woman with a shopping cart full of groceries cuts in line right in front of you. She says: "You don't mind if I cut in here, do you?" [Eisler, Hersen, Miller, & Blanchard, 1975, p. 332].*

The behavior was assessed in terms of the following variables.

Nonverbal behavior:
    Duration of eye contact
    Frequency of smiles
    Affect
    Duration of reply
    Fluency of response
    Loudness of speech
    Speech-disturbance ratio

Content measure:
    Compliance content
    Request for new behavior
    Praise
    Appreciation
    Spontaneous positive behavior

The responses of the subjects were videotaped and rated in terms of nonverbal behavior and content measure. Results indicated that the social context of interpersonal interaction was functionally related to the individual's behavior. In negative situations calling for "standing up for one's rights," the subjects evidenced greater assertion toward female partners than toward male partners. The subjects, however, were also more likely to offer praise and appreciation (positive assertion) to female than to male partners. Also, unfamiliar individuals, especially in positive contexts, elicited more assertion than familiar persons.

Eisler et al. (1975) stated:

> In general, the results support a stimulus-specific theory of assertiveness. That is, an individual who is assertive in one interpersonal context may not be assertive in a different interpersonal environment. Further, some individuals may have no difficulty responding with negative assertions but may be unable to respond when the situation requires positive expressions [p. 339].

These investigators also stressed the behavioral complexity of what is commonly referred to as "assertiveness," noting that ". . . assertive responding requires the coordinated delivery of numerous verbal and nonverbal responses" (p. 339). They found that high-assertive individuals talked longer, louder, and with greater affect but smiled less frequently. They noted, however, that, because of their particular subject population and its sociocultural background, as well as the nature of the assertive situations sampled, their findings could not be generalized. They stressed the need for additional research with different populations to also include women and concluded that

> . . . training individuals to be more reinforcing to others would appear to be indicated in a variety of clinical situations. Further, it is not likely that therapists can train clients "to be more assertive" in a general sense. Instead, clinicians should identify classes of interpersonal situations in which deficits can be identified. Training will then consist of increasing assertive responding to specific types of interactions with different individuals [p. 340].

Use of the Assertive Behavior Record Form

Before concluding this section on the behavioral procedures used in the development of assertive behavior, let's discuss once more the Assertive Behavior Record Form (ABRF), which we described in Chapter Four. This form can be used very effectively in determining behaviors that may benefit from rehearsal, modeling, or related procedures. Individuals undergoing assertive training are instructed to record on the form for a designated period of time—usually one week but sometimes throughout the entire assertive-training period—situations they encounter that make them uncomfortable because they are unable to handle them assertively.

   Since it is important that the individual have a clear understanding of what assertive behavior is, the therapist makes sure that the client knows the difference between assertive, nonassertive, and aggressive behavior. Then the therapist carefully checks all the situations the individual has described in the ABRF and points out any instance of inappropriate behavior. This serves as a continuing-education process for the patient. But the most valuable aspect of the use of the ABRF is that it provides material for behavioral rehearsal. Each response the individual has described in Column Three of the form (the response he would have liked to have made to the situation) is rehearsed before the therapist, who interacts with the individual as he rehearses and advises and coaches him as necessary. Eventually, as assertive training progresses, the therapist carefully refines the individual's behavior until it reaches the desired degree of assertiveness.

   Behavioral rehearsal doesn't, of course, have to be limited to the behaviors described on the ABRF. Other behaviors, suggested either by the individual or by the therapist, can and should be rehearsed. These may be situations that the individual has encountered in the past and found difficult to handle or anticipated situations that the person feels he is not able to handle appropriately. In addition, the ABRF may provide target behavior for use with the other procedures we have discussed in this chapter, such as modeling, role playing, and covert-conditioning techniques. The ABRF may also be used by the individual on his own. After therapy has progressed fairly far, the person may elect to rehearse some of the discomforting situations on his own. He may do this between therapy sessions as well as in the therapy sessions.

   The use of the ABRF also serves a useful purpose in the evaluation of the effectiveness of assertive training. As training nears completion, the therapist may ask the client to use the ABRF again. The form will provide the therapist with a means of checking if there are still situations that the client feels he cannot handle assertively. If this is the case, therapy continues; if not, or if the client's response is very close to the desired response, therapy may be terminated.

Suggested Readings

Bandura, A. (Ed.). *Psychological modeling: Conflicting theories.* Chicago: Aldine/Atherton, 1971.

Bergin, A. E., & Garfield, S. L. (Eds.). *Handbook of psychotherapy and behavior change: An empirical analysis.* New York: John Wiley & Sons, 1971.

Rimm, D. C., & Masters, J. C. *Behavior therapy: Techniques and empirical findings.* New York: Academic Press, 1974.

Thoresen, C. E., & Mahoney, M. J. *Behavioral self-control.* New York: Holt, Rinehart and Winston, 1974.

Watson, D. L., & Tharp, R. G. *Self-directed behavior: Self-modification for personal adjustment.* Monterey, Calif.: Brooks/Cole, 1972.

Wenrich, W. W., Dawley, H. H., & General, D. *Systematic desensitization: A guide for the client, student and therapist.* Kalamazoo, Mich.: Behaviordelia, 1976.

Chapter Seven / *Troubleshooting*

Topic Overview

I. Crisis situations may result from assertive behavior. Learning to cope with these situations is an important part of assertive training.

II. How do you handle someone who tries to make you feel guilty?

III. "Impossible" people—what do you do with them?

IV. When assertion does not work

V. Choosing not to assert yourself

VI. As you learn to become more assertive, you might, from time to time, act aggressively rather than assertively.

VII. Recovery after a fall

VIII. The rule for maintaining assertive behavior: Keep practicing assertive techniques!

This chapter examines various situations that can arise as you practice assertive behavior and offers some suggestions on ways of handling these situations—ways that should permit you to maintain and further develop an assertive life-style and, at the same time, successfully overcome the potentially negative consequences of your assertiveness.

Crisis Situations

One of the most important skills to be developed in the course of assertive training is the ability to handle crises. Obviously, no one can teach you how to handle all crisis situations; but there are some general guidelines that can help you become more adept at handling specific crisis situations relating to assertive behavior. Such situations may occur, for example, when someone responds in a totally inappropriate, often aggressive, manner to your assertive behavior.

Suppose that, as you learn to behave more assertively, you begin to interact more assertively with someone with whom you had previously interacted in a nonassertive manner. The other person may react rather strongly to your changed behavior and become very hostile—to the point of verbal or even physical abuse. This may be due to the fact that the other person is unable, at least at first, to handle the new situation adequately. The best thing you can do under the circumstances is to remain calm and refrain from answering hostility with hostility. You may tell the person you are sorry he feels so disturbed, but you should not let his response deter you from maintaining your assertive behavior. If the person continues to respond aggressively, you may again express your regret and your hope that at some later time both of you will be able to reexamine the issue and come to an understanding. The essential thing is that you continue to behave assertively, while, at the same time, avoiding a confrontation.

A person who refuses to listen to reason may be unable to deal with the situation in a rational manner and may seek a confrontation in order to interact with you in the only way he can—by verbal and/or physical abuse. In other words, either because of the particular situation or because of his personality, or both, the person may actually be "looking for trouble." It is prudent to keep these possibilities in mind when your assertive behavior fails to produce the desired results and you are confronted with this kind of overt hostility. Under the circumstances, you may choose to stop interacting with that person (if you can), but, as we said earlier, you should not let him deter you from behaving assertively or force you into a confrontation.

Since crises may arise in any number and kinds of situations, the development of pat responses for each potential crisis is neither possible nor desirable. Rather, you should be prepared for the possibility of such situations occurring and be able to handle them assertively and reasonably. Your goal is to become an assertive person. As we said at the beginning of this book, an assertive person is someone who has the ability to secure and maintain his or her rights without violating the rights of others. Implied in this definition is that you don't abuse others and you don't let others abuse you.

Dealing with Someone Who Tries to Make You Feel Guilty

Another situation you may encounter as you become more assertive is that of having to deal with people who try to make you feel guilty. As we said earlier, some people cannot handle, at least at first, a shift in your behavior that alters established relationship patterns. Some people may become hostile, and others may try to make you feel guilty because you don't give in as you used to. "You don't like me anymore, otherwise you would do what I ask of you" is a comment that you are likely to hear under these circumstances. It is also likely that, when this happens, you *will* feel uncomfortable and guilty. This is perfectly natural. But here, too, it is very important that you don't let the other person control you—in this case, through your own feelings. Tell yourself that it is foolish for you to feel guilty, since you didn't do anything to justify that feeling, and tell the other person, as firmly and kindly as you can, the reasons for your behavior, stressing that your "not liking him (or her) anymore" is certainly not one of them. This may work or not. If it doesn't, you may want to try again, but, if you fail, you may be left with only one choice— letting that person go. One of the prices you must be prepared to pay for a more rewarding life-style is that you may have to relinquish relationships that cannot stand the test of your assertive behavior.

An example of this situation will perhaps make our points clearer.

The Case of Charles

Charles has been successfully working for some time toward developing a more effective style of personal interaction. Things have been going pretty smoothly, when one day he tries to behave assertively with Don, who, caught by surprise, doesn't know how to handle Charles's unexpected firmness and—although recognizing that Charles is right—reacts with anger and hostility. In order to discourage his friend's assertive behavior, Don tries to convince Charles that he has been aggressive, that he has unjustly hurt him, and that he should feel sorry for having abused their friendship.

Charles is shocked. Although he feels he was right and Don's reaction is uncalled for, he thinks the whole matter over and carefully considers their respective views. To obtain a better perspective, he places himself in the position of an outside observer and again looks at his own behavior. Still not completely satisfied, Charles seeks an unbiased outside opinion by describing the situation to an uninvolved third party. All these steps confirm Charles in his opinion that his behavior was justified, but they also give him an indication of how some of it could have been misperceived by Don. He resolves to make an effort next time to present things in such a way as to leave no room for "misperceptions" on Don's part, but he feels assured that he was basically correct; therefore he is able to think of his relationship with Don and of the recent upsetting incident without feeling guilty.

"Impossible" People

We all know people with whom it is almost impossible to interact in a mode of mutual respect. At work, in school, or in a social setting, the "impossible" person crosses our path and confronts us with a problem that is often difficult to solve.

Handling impossible people varies, of course, from situation to situation. In some cases, a direct approach may be quite appropriate; in others, a more subtle approach is advisable. With certain people we may have no hesitation expressing our feelings; with others—for example, a supervisor or someone with whom we have to interact daily—we would be wise to be more cautious. What we are saying is that here, too, there are no hard-and-fast rules that apply to all situations. The guiding principle should be a judicious balance between the value of assertiveness and the weight of its potentially negative consequences—for example, aggravating an already poor situation.

Short of just walking away from "impossible" people, you may, if feasible, communicate your feelings by telling them that you find their behavior upsetting and that you don't enjoy being with them when they behave that way. But you should also keep in mind that, at one time or another, you will encounter people with whom you simply cannot interact adequately.

When Assertion Does Not Work

Earlier in the book, we indicated that effective communication and meaningful relationships are likely to result from assertiveness. And yet the chances are that, as you practice assertive behavior, sooner or later you are going to run into a situation in which assertiveness, instead of improving communication, causes communication to break down. This may be due, of course, to your asserting yourself inappropriately; but more often it is the result of the other person's inability to deal with your assertive behavior. Since learning how to cope with this problem is a very important part of assertive training, we shall direct a fair amount of attention to this issue.

What do you do if you have, to the best of your knowledge, assertively and clearly expressed your feelings and thoughts to a friend (whom we shall call Eleanor), but she reacts negatively and fails to effectively communicate the reason for her displeasure to you? Eleanor may, for real or imagined reasons, believe that your assertion was unwarranted and, as a result, view it as an instance of offensive (rather than assertive) behavior; or she may understand exactly what you are saying, realize the legitimacy of your claim, but be unable to handle the situation appropriately. Instead of telling you openly how she feels and trying to come to an understanding, she responds aggressively.

This aggression may be expressed in rather subtle ways, such as ignoring you, not talking to you, or engaging in "smiling hostility." If you are one of those people who are not bothered beyond endurance by this kind of behavior, a good way of handling the situation is to continue interacting as normally as possible until, with time, Eleanor overcomes her ill feelings toward you and begins to interact more normally. If, on the other hand, you find "smiling hostility" and being ignored difficult to handle, more direct action on your part is called for.

What are your options? First of all, since the outcome of this kind of situation is generally a breakdown of communication, low-keyed efforts toward reestablishing communication represent a first step in the right direction. Because Eleanor has elected to ignore you as much as possible, you should limit your overtures to business and other impersonal topics (as opposed to "small talk," which may give her the uncomfortable feeling that she is compelled to answer). In many instances, this approach works, since it is likely to get communication going again, which in turn leads to a return to the normal interactional mode of behavior.

In those occasions in which it is difficult or impossible to initiate communication, more direct behavior on your part may be called for. Realizing again that in personal interactions assertiveness is generally the most effective approach overall, you may decide to come right out and confront Eleanor again. You should do this at what you consider to be an opportune time and tell her that you feel that her behavior toward you is uncalled for. You may then again explain why you feel that your original assertive statements were legitimate and, depending on Eleanor's reactions, go on to express your regret that your views upset her. At the very least, this approach should serve to let Eleanor vent some of the pent-up hostility she has been harboring since your initial assertiveness. You may help this release of emotion by encouraging her to clarify her comments reflecting her feelings and, more generally, by assisting her to "get it all out." You may then elect to say that you think you understand (if you do understand) how she feels, express your regret again, but remain firm about the legitimacy of your stand. This interchange should clear the air of bottled-up emotions and misunderstandings and make it possible for you and Eleanor to interact again in a normal fashion.

What about those situations in which none of the above approaches work? Well, as we said earlier, the fact that assertive behavior may not always work is something you must accept. As you keep asserting yourself, you will see that the rewards of assertiveness far exceed its drawbacks. The high rate of success that will mark your assertive interactions with others should confirm that assertiveness helps you communicate better and thus establish more meaningful relationships, even if, once in a while, you may have to face unpleasant situations. Incidentally, as you progress in your assertive training, you may find it helpful to rehearse or role-play situations in which your assertion does not produce the desired results.

The Case of Patricia

Patricia is an ambitious young university instructor, well liked and respected by her students and colleagues. Another faculty member—an older man named Lou—has developed the habit of asking Patricia to account to him. Lou, who is the senior member of Patricia's department, has come to look on the department as his personal domain. At one time, Lou handled many of the functions of the department chairman, and since then he has felt his duty to "put new professors in their place."

Patricia's turn for being "put in her place" came when Lou began questioning her about her use of time during school hours, which, in Patricia's view, amounted to his asking her to account for herself. Patricia was secure in the knowledge that she was handling her classes and office hours properly, and, since she informed the chairman when she was off campus for significant periods of time, Lou's insistence that she account to him for her time caused Patricia to become increasingly irritated.

As her annoyance mounted, Patricia asked herself what she should do. Should she say nothing and put up with what she saw as an infringement of her rights? Should she simply tell Lou to mind his own business and then ignore him? Or should she go further and tell him that he had no right to question her and, moreover, that he had no real authority in the department? Patricia had a hard time deciding on her course. On the one hand, Lou had many good qualities and she didn't want to jeopardize what she felt was basically a good friendly relationship; on the other hand, Lou could be fairly aggressive and hostile if he felt like it, and Patricia had seen him make it uncomfortable for others who had angered him.

One day, after she was gone for an unusually long time, Lou came on pretty strong asking her, in a peremptory manner, for a detailed explanation of where she had been. Reacting to her accumulated irritation, Patricia took this opportunity (not the most appropriate occasion, in view of her long absence) to assert herself. Noting that his interrogations were apparently based on his view that she must account to him, she observed that her position as a member of the faculty did not require her to account to a fellow faculty member. In passing, she noted that this time Lou might have a legitimate reason for inquiring about her absence, simply because it had been an unusually long one. However, she emphasized that, on most of the other occasions, she felt that he had been infringing on her rights. Since her primary aim was to communicate effectively, Patricia attempted to convey her feelings in a nonhostile, nonthreatening manner.

Lou's reaction was to focus solely on her recent absence, and he emphatically stated that his inquiry was justified. Patricia, recognizing the possible legitimacy of his view, agreed and iterated that he might have been justified in that case but also noted again the many occasions in which she felt he had infringed on her rights. Lou, incensed over what he perceived as an attack, reacted with anger, restating once again his conviction that he was correct in asking her to account for her last absence. And, again, Patricia said *yes*, this was possibly an appropriate instance, *but* what she was objecting to were the other occasions in which she felt he had infringed on her rights. After a few more exchanges along the same lines, the discussion was terminated amicably—or so Patricia believed. In fact, she felt pleased that she had appropriately asserted herself without jeopardizing a valued relationship.

Lou, on the other hand, chose to perceive Patricia's "attack" as an assertion that she could come and go as she pleased and didn't have to account to anybody, and he completely ignored her comments on the legitimacy of his last inquiry. The more Lou thought about the incident, the more incensed he became, and finally he chose to express his anger in a passive manner by simply not talking to Patricia. Patricia did not realize Lou's anger and resentment until the next day, when she joined a conversation with Lou and other faculty members and Lou pointedly ignored her. Patricia left the group with the realization that her assertiveness of the previous day had not produced the desired results; instead of the expected positive outcome, she was now confronted with a negative situation in the form of passive aggression.

Patricia considered what she should do. Should she simply wait for Lou to get over his irritation? Should she attempt to reestablish communication? Or should she respond in kind and also behave in a passive aggressive manner? But, since being ignored made Patricia extremely anxious and interfered with her work and her relationships with others—a characteristic she was well aware of— Patricia decided to attempt to reestablish communication with Lou. The problem was how to get communication going again without running the risk of making things worse. She felt that she had already adequately asserted herself and that the problem lay with Lou's inability to handle his feelings.

With this in mind, Patricia approached Lou and attempted to convey two points: (1) that she clearly differentiated between his recent and possibly legitimate inquiry about her last absence and his previous questions, which she felt had infringed on her privacy, and (2) that she regretted any discomfort she had caused as a result of her assertion. Then Patricia asked Lou if he was purposefully ignoring her. Lou responded by restating that he had been right in inquiring about her last absence. Patricia agreed that he had been right in that case and that case only and once again expressed regret over any discomfort she might have caused. Lou clearly appreciated her expression of regret and firmly denied that he was ignoring her. As a result of this interchange, Patricia and Lou re-established a relationship that was characterized by mutual respect.

Patricia's assertive behavior produced an unexpected and uncomfortable problem; her method of resolving that problem is a good example of one possible way of handling some of the unexpected results of assertion.

Choosing Not to Assert Yourself

Recall that in Chapter Three we made a distinction between people who are unable to assert themselves and people who, under certain circumstances, elect not to assert themselves. There are indeed situations in which the wise course of action is that of avoiding an assertive stand. The governing factor in your decision should be the evaluation of the seriousness of the potentially negative consequences of your assertive behavior. If, in a particular situation, you believe that the liabilities of an assertive act far outweigh the possible rewards, you may choose—and wisely so—not to assert yourself. But the key word here is "choose"; that is, you are capable of behaving assertively, but you choose not to. Of central importance is the fact that the decision not to assert yourself is yours alone.

Each situation is different, and each has its own unique factors that need to be considered in deciding what might be the most appropriate behavior. In certain instances, before making your decision, you may want to ask yourself a few questions, such as "Is the person under a great deal of stress?" "Are there other reasons that could explain his behavior and that I may not be aware of?" and, simply, "Is it worth it, under the circumstances?" Depending on the answers you find to your questions, you may then elect to assert or not. If you have already asserted yourself, you may choose to stop asserting yourself with that person—completely or in the specific instance.

How you manage the situation depends of course on the particular nature of your relationship with the person, the specific circumstances, and your overall feelings about the possible outcome of various strategies. Depending on your degree of discomfort and desire to normalize the relationship, you may make one or several conciliatory moves, including, on appropriate occasions, going out of your way to give a greeting or pay a compliment. A risk involved in this procedure is that the other person may interpret your conciliatory move as an act of subservience—a tacit acknowledgment on your part that your initial assertion was wrong. If you find this eventuality intolerable because in your eyes it would amount to giving in to unwarranted behavior, then you may choose not to make this kind, or any kind, of conciliatory move. This is, of course, your decision to make. If you cannot or do not want to make conciliatory moves, you may bear with the status quo, in the hope that eventually the situation will normalize itself. As we have said many times before, it will be easier for you to take a situational setback if you realize and accept that assertion may not always have the desired results and, consequently, that other adaptive behavior may be required. Keep trying. If you behave adaptively and assertively, the immediate and long-term personal gains will far outweigh the negative consequences.

Temporary Aggressiveness during Assertive Training

In the preceding pages, our focus has been on how you can handle the inadaptive responses of others to your assertive behavior. Before concluding our discussion, we should spend a little time on the possibility of unadaptive behavior on *your* part as you learn to become more assertive.

Overly sensitive, inhibited individuals find it extremely difficult to assert themselves. When they do begin to behave assertively and thus discover that they *can* do it, they may for a period of time go too far in the other direction—that is, swing from nonassertiveness to obnoxiousness and even aggressiveness. They enjoy freedom of expression and release from confining restraints perhaps for the first time in their lives, and these newly discovered, exhilarating feelings can make a person mistake aggressiveness for assertiveness. As we have stressed many times in the course of this book, this mistake can have very negative consequences and lead to emotionally laden crisis situations that are very difficult to handle. It is therefore important that, as you undergo assertive training, you keep monitoring your behavior all the time to be sure that you are relating assertively and not aggressively. Using the "outside observer" approach to ask yourself how others would view your behavior is, as we have seen, an effective monitoring procedure. The therapist himself, if you are working under the guidance of one, can help you by being alert to any problem situations that may come up as a result of your being aggressive rather than assertive and by making sure that you are always aware of the true nature of your behavior.

Recovery after a Fall

Most of us find it very difficult to be assertive when we are afraid, depressed, or anxious. There are days in which we just don't feel like saying anything to anybody—especially something assertive. These moods are often the result of frustrating experiences that, because of the acute discomfort they cause, make us oversensitive, guarded, and anxious. Anger and hostility remain unexpressed and thus compound the problem. This pattern is particularly characteristic of nonassertive individuals. During assertive training, they may go weeks or months before encountering a situation that they cannot handle successfully; but when such a situation develops, they don't seem to be able to take it. Their self-esteem crumbles, and they are filled with anger and hostility (generally unexpressed) toward the individual who, intentionally or unintentionally, said or did something that was perceived as calling for an assertive response. Incidents of this nature can trigger extremely unwholesome reactions and cause great discomfort. They may occur at any time during assertive training, but their frequency tends to decrease as assertive training progresses. But no matter how frequent, these situations are uncomfortable, and the individual should be cautioned that they may occur and that he or she should be prepared to face them and, hopefully, handle them successfully.

Maintaining Assertive Behavior

Individuals in need of assertive training often seriously misperceive what goes on in any given personal interaction. What is appropriately assertive behavior on their part is likely to evoke feelings of guilt, fear, and remorse, because these individuals cannot easily accept the fact that interacting assertively is healthy and because they often have a lifetime history of inhibitions that have resulted in a variety of self-imposed controls. When they undergo assertive training, these people begin to assert themselves and to accept the view that assertive behavior is likely to bring about effective communication and good interpersonal relationships. But, unless they keep practicing assertive techniques, they cannot establish a lasting pattern of assertiveness; their initial gains are likely to remain just gallant but temporary attempts at adopting a more adaptive style of behavior. Therefore, if you are working toward becoming a more assertive person, *keep practicing assertive techniques;* practice them until they become a natural part of your behavioral repertoire. With time, the positive reinforcement that follows assertive behavior will increase and will eventually maintain your assertive style.

Most people who seek the help of a therapist for assertive training do so because they have problems that cause them acute discomfort. Consequently, they enter therapy with a very high level of motivation. This is, at least potentially, a time in which a great deal of work can be done, although a balance must be maintained between the advantage of capitalizing on the high drive level and the danger of going through assertive training too fast. Incidentally, these periods of acute discomfort are not limited to the time immediately preceding training; they may also flare up from time to time after training has begun. But no matter how high or low the degree of discomfort is, individuals undergoing assertive training must *consistently* relate assertively, even if, from time to time, they may choose not to assert themselves. As we have seen, it is all right not to assert oneself, if one *chooses* to do so; the option to assert oneself or not must always be there.

After assertive training has been completed, the person may periodically relapse into nonassertiveness in response to anxiety or other inhibiting factors. If this pattern continues, it could lead right back to the original unadaptive mode of behavior. Although you don't have to assert yourself on each and every occasion, you should be alert to the possibility of regressive nonassertiveness and know the techniques you can employ in order to maintain an appropriately assertive repertoire.

As a final note, we wish to repeat once again that assertive behavior is positive, healthy, and rewarding behavior. It frees you from the negative and destructive feelings of low self-esteem, of anger toward yourself, of hostility toward others, and of the despair that comes from being unable to get what is rightly yours. Assertive behavior makes you feel good about yourself, helps you establish and maintain meaningful and fulfilling relationships, and, more generally, gives you a real chance to live your life as a better and richer person.

References

Alberti, R. E., & Emmons, M. L. *Your perfect right: A guide to assertive behavior.* San Luis Obispo, Calif.: Impact, 1970.

Bandura, A. (Ed.). *Psychological modeling: Conflicting theories.* Chicago: Aldine/ Atherton, 1971. (a)

Bandura, A. Psychotherapy based upon modeling principles. In A. E. Bergin & S. L. Garfield (Eds.), *Handbook of psychotherapy and behavior change: An empirical analysis.* New York: John Wiley & Sons, 1971. (b)

Bergin, A. E., & Garfield, S. L. (Eds.). *Handbook of psychotherapy and behavior change: An empirical analysis.* New York: John Wiley & Sons, 1971.

Ciminero, A. R., Calhoun, K. S., & Adams, H. E. (Eds.). *Handbook of behavioral assessment.* New York: John Wiley & Sons, in press.

Deibert, A. N., & Harmon, A. J. *New tools for changing behavior.* Champaign, Ill.: Research Press, 1972.

Eisenson, J. *The improvement of voice and diction.* New York: Macmillan, 1958.

Eisler, R. M., Hersen, M., & Miller, P. M. Effects of modeling on components of assertive behavior. *Journal of Behavior Therapy and Experimental Psychiatry,* 1973, 4(1), 1-6.

Eisler, R. M., Hersen M., Miller, P. M., & Blanchard, E. B. Situational determinants of assertive behavior. *Journal of Consulting and Clinical Psychology,* 1975, 43(3), 330-340.

Eisler, R. M., Miller, P. M., & Hersen, M. Components of assertive behavior. *Journal of Clinical Psychology,* 1973, 29(3), 295-299.

Ellis, A. *Healthy and unhealthy aggression.* Paper presented at the 81st Annual Convention of the American Psychological Association, Montreal, August 1973.

Ford, H., & Urban, H. *Systems of psychotherapy: A comparative study.* New York: John Wiley & Sons, 1963.

Friedman, P. H. The effects of modeling and role playing on assertive behavior. In R. D. Rubin, H. Fensterheim, A. A. Lazarus, & C. M. Franks (Eds.), *Advances in behavior therapy.* New York: Academic Press, 1971.

Galassi, J. P., Delo, J. S., Galassi, M. D., & Bastein, S. The college self-expression scale: A measure of assertiveness. *Behavior Therapy,* 1974, 5, 165-171.

Galassi, J. P., Galassi, M. D., & Litz, M. C. Assertive training in groups using video feedback. *Journal of Counseling Psychology,* 1974, 21, 390-394.

Gay, M. L., Hollandsworth, J. G., & Galassi, J. P. An assertiveness inventory for adults. *Journal of Counseling Psychology,* 1975, 22, 340-344.

Hersen, M., & Bellack, A. S. Assessment of social skills. In A. R. Ciminero, K. S. Calhoun, & H. E. Adams (Eds.), *Handbook of behavioral assessment.* New York: John Wiley & Sons, in press.

Hersen, M., Eisler, R. M., & Miller, P. M. Development of assertive responses: Clinical, measurement, and research considerations. *Behaviour Research and Therapy,* 1973, *11,* 505–522.

Hersen, M., Eisler, R. M., Miller, P. M., Johnson, M. B., & Pinkston, S. G. Effects of practice, instruction and modeling on components of assertive behavior. *Behaviour Research and Therapy,* 1973, *11*(4), 443–451.

Jacobson, E. *Progressive relaxation.* Chicago: University of Chicago Press, 1938.

Karoly, P., & Kanfer, F. H. Situational and historical determinants of self-reinforcement. *Behavior Therapy,* 1974, *5,* 381–390.

Kazdin, A. E. Effects of covert modeling and model reinforcement of assertive behavior. *Journal of Abnormal Psychology,* 1974, *83*(3), 240–252.

Kazdin, A. E. Covert modeling, imagery assessment, and assertive behavior. *Journal of Consulting and Clinical Psychology,* 1975, *43*(5), 716–724.

Laws, D. R., & Serber, M. *Measurement and evaluation of assertive training with sexual offenders.* Paper presented at the Annual Meeting of the Association for the Advancement of Behavior Therapy, Washington, D.C., 1971.

Lazarus, A. A. Behaviour rehearsal vs. non-directive therapy vs. advice in effecting behaviour change. *Behaviour Research and Therapy,* 1966, *4,* 209–212.

Lazarus, A. A. *Behavior therapy and beyond.* New York: McGraw-Hill, 1971.

Lazarus, A. A. *Daily living: Coping with tension and anxieties.* Chicago: Instructional Dynamics, 1972.

Lazarus, A. A. On assertive behavior: A brief note. *Behavior Therapy,* 1973.

MacPherson, E. L. Selective operant conditioning and deconditioning of assertive modes of behavior. *Journal of Behavior Therapy and Experimental Psychiatry,* 1972, *3*(2), 99–102.

Malott, R., Ritterby, K., & Wolf, E. L. *An introduction to behavior modification.* Kalamazoo, Mich.: Behaviordelia, 1973.

Malott, R., & Whaley, D. *Psychology.* New York: Behaviordelia/Harper & Row, 1976.

McFall, R. M., & Lillesand, D. B. Behavior rehearsal with modeling and coaching in assertion training. *Journal of Abnormal Psychology,* 1971, *77,* 313–323.

McFall, R. M., & Marston, A. R. An experimental investigation of behavior rehearsal in assertive training. *Journal of Abnormal Psychology,* 1970, *76,* 295–303.

McFall, R. M., & Twentyman, C. T. Four experiments on the relative contributions of rehearsal, modeling, and coaching to assertion training. *Journal of Abnormal Psychology,* 1973, *81*(3), 199–218.

Rachman, S. *The effects of psychotherapy.* Oxford: Pergamon Press, 1971.

Rathus, S. A. An experimental investigation of assertive training in a group setting. *Journal of Behavior Therapy and Experimental Psychiatry,* 1972, *3,* 81–86.

Rathus, S. A. A 30-item schedule for assessing assertive behavior. *Behavior Therapy,* 1973, *4,* 398–406. (a)

Rathus, S. A. Instigation of assertive behaviour through videotaped-mediated assertive models and directed practice. *Behaviour Research and Therapy,* 1973, *11,* 57–65. (b)

Rimm, D. C., & Masters, J. C. *Behavior therapy: Techniques and empirical findings.* New York: Academic Press, 1974.

Salter, A. *Conditioned reflex therapy.* New York: Farrar, Strauss, 1949.

Serber, M. Teaching the non-verbal components of assertive training. *Journal of Behavior Therapy and Experimental Psychiatry,* 1972, *3*(3), 179–183.

Thoresen, C. E., & Mahoney, M. J. *Behavioral self-control*. New York: Holt, Rinehart and Winston, 1974.

Watson, D. L., & Tharp, R. G. *Self-directed behavior: Self-modification for personal adjustment*. Monterey, Calif.: Brooks/Cole, 1972.

Wenrich, W. W. *A primer of behavior modification*. Monterey, Calif.: Brooks/Cole, 1970.

Wenrich, W. W., Dawley, H. H., & General, D. *Self-directed systematic desensitization: A guide for the student, client, and therapist*. Kalamazoo, Mich.: Behaviordelia, 1976.

Whaley, D. L., & Malott, R. *Elementary principles of behavior*. New York: Appleton-Century-Crofts, 1971.

Wolpe, J. *Psychotherapy by reciprocal inhibition*. Stanford, Calif.: Stanford University Press, 1958.

Wolpe, J. *The practice of behavior therapy*. New York: Pergamon Press, 1969.

Wolpe, J. *The practice of behavior therapy* (2nd ed.). Oxford: Pergamon Press, 1973.

Wolpe, J., & Lazarus, A. A. *Behavior therapy techniques: A guide to the treatment of neuroses*. New York: Pergamon Press, 1966.

Appendix A
Muscle relaxation exercises*

Introduction

The basic idea of these exercises is to teach you how to relax fully and completely. It has been found that an effective method of achieving relaxation is to tense the various muscles and muscle groups of your body as tightly as you can, holding and studying the tension for a few moments, and then releasing the tension and noticing the difference. The idea is to methodically concentrate on the difference between tension and relaxation. While tensing any specified area of your body the rest of your body should remain as relaxed as possible. As you progress through these exercises, you will learn to enjoy the relaxation more and more as it becomes deeper and more complete. Throughout these exercises, you will notice a series of three dots (. . .). These dots indicate periods where you are to pause for five or ten seconds and concentrate on the sensations you are feeling at that moment.

General Loosening Up

These exercises are designed to loosen up your major muscles and will take about two or three minutes. Begin by standing up and stretching your hands over your head as high as you can, stretching all of the muscles from your finger tips down to your toes. Hold this tension for a few moments . . . then relax . . . Repeat this exercise several times. Now bend forward, tensing the muscles along your back and legs . . . study the tension for a few moments . . . then relax and notice the difference . . . repeat this exercise several times. Next, lightly shake your hands and arms for a few seconds, relaxing all the muscles that you can. Then be seated, preferably in a comfortable, reclined lounge chair, and carry out the following exercises.

*These exercises are paraphrased to some extent from the relaxation exercises contained in *Behavior Therapy Techniques*, by Joseph Wolpe and Arnold Lazarus (New York: Pergamon Press, 1966), and are reprinted by permission from *Self-Directed Systematic Desensitization: A Guide for the Student, Client, and Therapist*, by W. W. Wenrich, H. H. Dawley, and D. General. Copyright 1976 by Behaviordelia.

Development of Relaxation in the
Hands and Arms

These exercises will take approximately four to six minutes to complete. You should, at this point, already be seated with both feet comfortably extended out in front of you, your arms and hands resting along the arms of the chair, and your head and neck in a relaxed, resting position. Relax like this for a few moments . . . now, make your right hand into a tight fist, clench your fist tight—as tightly as you can—and build up the tension in your hand and forearm . . . study this tension for a few moments . . . now relax and notice the difference . . . once more, clench your right fist as tightly as you can, build up the tension, study it . . . now relax and notice the difference . . . now clench your left hand and make it into a tight fist. Make the fist tighter and tighter, build up the tension and study it for a few moments . . . now relax and notice the difference . . . once more, make your left hand into a tight fist, build up the tension in your hand and forearm tighter and tighter, study this tension for a few moments . . . and now relax and notice the difference . . . notice how relaxed your hands are and how much more pleasant the relaxation is compared to tension. Concentrate on relaxing all over for a few moments . . . next, bend your right elbow, making your right hand into a fist and tensing your forearm and upper arm as tight as you can, build up this tension tighter and tighter, study it for a few moments . . . now relax . . . straighten your arm and let the tension flow out . . . notice the difference between the tension and relaxation . . . enjoy the relaxation for a few moments . . . now, once more, bend your right elbow, making your right hand into a fist and building up the tension in your hand, forearm, and upper arm. Build up this tension and study it for a few moments . . . now relax . . . straighten out your arm and hand and let all the tension flow out. Concentrate on studying the difference between relaxation and tension . . . now breathe normally and rest for a few moments . . . next, bend your left elbow, making your left hand into a fist, and tightly tense your forearm and upper arm, build up the tension in your upper arm, study it . . . now relax and notice the difference . . . notice how good the absence of tension feels . . . enjoy this relaxation for a few moments . . . now, once again, bend your left elbow very hard, making your left hand into a tight fist and your upper arm muscle into a tight ball, build up the tension as much as you can . . . study the tension . . . now relax and notice the difference . . . let all the tension flow out of your muscles and concentrate on becoming as relaxed as you can . . . just concentrate on relaxing as completely as you can, and remain in this position as the instructions for the next relaxation exercises begin . . .

Development of Relaxation in the Neck,
Face, and Shoulders

These exercises will take about four to six minutes to complete. Take a few moments and continue resting . . . now let your head roll slowly around for a few turns as loosely as you can . . . next turn your head to the right as far as you can, building up the tension and studying it . . . now relax and notice the difference . . . notice how good the absence of tension feels . . . now repeat this procedure once more. Turn your head to the right as far as you can, build up the tension and study it for a few moments . . . now relax and notice the difference . . . next, turn your head to the left as far as you can . . . build up the tension and study it . . . now relax, let all the tension flow out, and concentrate on studying the difference . . . once again, turn your head to the left as far as you can, build up the tension, study it . . . now relax and notice the difference . . . now bend your head forward, pressing your chin against your chest as tightly as you can, build up the tension . . . study it . . . now relax and notice the difference . . . next, concentrate on relaxing your shoulders. Begin by shrugging or bringing your shoulders up as tightly as you can, build up the tension, study it . . . now relax and notice the difference . . . let all the tension flow away . . . relax all the muscles in your neck and shoulders . . . relax all over as fully as you can . . . continue relaxing for a while . . .

Now concentrate on relaxing your facial muscles. Begin by frowning and furrowing your brow as tightly as you can, build up the tension . . . study it . . . now relax and notice the difference . . . once more, frown and furrow your brow as tightly as you can, build up the tension . . . study it . . . now relax and notice the difference . . . next, move on to your eyes and, closing them, squint them as tightly as you can, build up the tension . . . study it . . . now relax and notice the difference . . . once again, close your eyes and squint them tightly, build up the tension . . . study it for a few moments . . . now relax and notice the difference . . . let all the muscles in your forehead, around your eyes, and all over your face and entire body relax as fully as you can . . . move on to your lips and tongue. Relax your lips by first pursing them tightly, build up the tension, study it . . . now release the tension and relax . . . notice the difference . . . once more, pucker your lips tight, build up the tension . . . study it . . . now relax and notice the difference . . . now press your tongue against the roof of your mouth, build up the tension and study it for a few moments . . . now relax and notice the difference . . . once more, press your tongue tightly up against the roof of your mouth . . . build up the tension . . . study it . . . now, relax and notice the difference . . . notice how much better the relaxation feels in contrast to the tension . . . now, concentrate on relaxing all the muscles in your neck, shoulders, and face . . . let all the tension flow out . . . relax deeper and deeper . . . continue relaxing for a while . . .

Relaxation of Upper Back, Chest, and Stomach

These exercises will last four to six minutes. Keeping the rest of your body relaxed, tense the muscles in your upper back area by raising your shoulders and shrugging them back and up; tense them tight, build up the tension . . . study it . . . now relax. Let your shoulders fall down and relax as completely as you can . . . notice all the tension flowing out of your upper back area . . . let yourself become more and more relaxed as the relaxation spreads throughout your entire body . . . now once again, tense the muscles in your upper back area by shrugging your shoulders up and back, build up the tension . . . study it . . . now relax, let your shoulders fall, and, as they do, let all the tension flow out of your body . . . let yourself become more and more relaxed . . . concentrate on experiencing this relaxation fully . . . concentrate on reducing even the slightest bit of tension . . . continue to relax and enjoy this feeling for a few moments.

Now, as you are relaxing, breathe in deeply, filling your lungs as fully as you can and hold it for a moment . . . exhale, breathe normally a few seconds while concentrating on relaxing more . . . breathe in deeply and again completely fill your lungs; then hold your breath for a few moments . . . now exhale and slowly permit the air to leave your lungs, concentrate on experiencing the increasing relaxation as you slowly exhale . . . breathe normally for a while, letting yourself become more and more relaxed . . . enjoy this spreading relaxation as you breathe in and out . . . now once again, breathe in deeply, fill your lungs, and hold your breath for a few moments. Study the sensation . . . now exhale slowly and concentrate on the pleasant experiences as you do . . . breathe normally again for a while, each time letting yourself become more and more relaxed . . . once more, breathe in deeply and fill your lungs to capacity; hold your breath for a few moments. Study the tension . . . now exhale slowly, concentrating on becoming more and more relaxed . . . let this relaxation spread throughout your entire body . . . your upper and lower back, shoulders, neck, face, chest, and arms are all becoming more and more relaxed as you breathe . . . as you continue breathing, concentrate on becoming more and more relaxed . . .

As the relaxation goes deeper and deeper, center your attention on your stomach and abdominal area. Pull in your stomach and make it and your entire abdominal area as tight as you can, build up this tension, and study it . . . now relax and let all the tension flow out of these muscles . . . notice how relaxed and loose your muscles are . . . let yourself become more and more relaxed . . . once again, pull in your stomach and make your abdominal muscles as tight as you can, build up this tension, study it . . . now release the tension and notice the difference . . . once more pull in your stomach and make your abdominal muscles as tight as you can. Study this tension for a few moments . . . now relax, releasing all of the tension in your stomach and abdominal muscles . . . continue relaxing for a few moments . . . next, inhale deeply and, pushing your diaphragm down, extend your stomach and tense your abdominal muscles as tight as you can. Study this tension . . . now exhale and relax, releasing all the tension from your stomach and abdominal muscles . . . enjoy this relaxation for a few moments . . . once more, inhale deeply and pushing your diaphragm down, extend your stomach and tense your abdominal muscles as tightly as you can, study this tension . . . now exhale and relax, releasing all the tension from your stomach and abdominal muscles . . . enjoy the ever-decreasing tension . . . continue breathing in and out for a while, concentrating on becoming more and more relaxed . . . let all the tension flow out of the muscles in your abdominal area as well as in the rest of your body

. . . as your muscles become more and more relaxed, you feel warm and somewhat sleepy . . . your eyelids are becoming heavier and it is hard to keep them open.

Relaxation Exercises for the Lower Back,
Hips, Thighs, and Calves

These exercises will last approximately four to six minutes. As your relaxation continues, pay attention next to your lower back. First arch your lower back, and tense the muscles there as tightly as you can, build up the tension, study it . . . now, relax and notice the difference . . . concentrate on relaxing your lower back as completely as you can . . . make your entire body more and more relaxed . . . deeper and deeper . . . once again, arch up your lower back and tense the muscles there as tightly as you can, study this tension for a few moments . . . now relax and notice the difference . . . next, tense the muscles in your buttocks, thighs, hips, legs, and calves by flexing your buttocks as tightly as you can while at the same time pressing down on the heels of your feet, exerting as much pressure as you can . . . build up this tension . . . study it . . . now, relax and notice the difference . . . concentrate on relaxing all of your muscles, deeper and deeper . . . once again flex your buttocks and press down hard on your heels, build up the tension . . . study it . . . now, relax and notice the difference . . . enjoy this relaxation for a few moments . . . next, while resting the heels of your feet, point your toes toward your head and tense all the muscles in your feet, ankles, and lower legs, build up this tension . . . study it . . . now relax and once more notice the difference; notice how good the relaxation feels. Once more, point your toes toward your head and tense all of the muscles in your feet, ankles, and lower legs. Build up this tension . . . study it . . . now relax and notice the difference . . . notice how soothing the relaxation is . . . let this relaxation spread throughout your body. Enjoy this relaxation for a while . . .

Final Relaxation and Instructions

Continue to rest and relax as you go through the final set of instructions. These instructions are intended to enhance and intensify the general overall state of deep muscle relaxation already achieved. They will last approximately two to six minutes. By now all of your muscles should be fairly well relaxed. Your eyelids feel heavy, your arms feel heavy, and you feel a warm sensation in all parts of your body along with a desire to fall asleep . . . now enhance your relaxation even more by again taking a deep breath, filling your lungs completely, and holding this tension for a few moments . . . then relax and slowly exhale . . . notice how relaxing it is as you exhale . . . breathe normally for a while and concentrate on going into a deeper state of relaxation . . . now once again, breathe in deeply, fill your lungs to maximum capacity, and hold your breath for a few moments . . . study the tension . . . now exhale slowly and notice the increased relaxation as you do so . . . breathe normally for a while, and concentrate on eliminating any tension anywhere in your body . . . as you breathe in and out, you will become more and more relaxed . . . the relaxation will go deeper and deeper . . . now once again breathe in deeply and fill your lungs to capacity . . . now hold your breath for a few moments and study the tension . . . now relax and notice the increased relaxation . . . continue breathing normally for a while and, as you do, you become even more and more relaxed . . . deeper and deeper . . . you should now be in a state of complete relaxation . . . enjoy and appreciate the very warm, pleasant, and comfortable experience of complete relaxation.

Appendix B
Assertive behavior record form

Date	Situation	Assertive Response

Date	Situation	Assertive Response

Date	Situation	Assertive Response

Date	Situation	Assertive Response

Date	Situation	Assertive Response

Date	Situation	Assertive Response

Index

Acceptance, 21
Active disagreement, 57, 65–66
Adams, H. E., 47, 101
Adaptive behavior, 15–29
Admiration, 55
Affection, 54, 55, 86
Affective reeducation, 53
Agreement, indiscriminate, 57
Aggression, 23–24, 45, 94 (*see also* Aggressiveness)
   defined, 23
Aggressiveness, 16, 18, 23–29
   general, 25–29
   situational, 25–29
   temporary, 98–99
Alberti, R. E., 21, 101
Alienation, 16
American Psychological Association, 24
Amplification, 51
Anger, 7, 22, 45, 52, 85, 86, 99, 100
Annoyance, 24
Antecedent condition, 10
Anxiety, 3, 7, 12, 20, 22, 61, 68, 70, 80, 99
   chronic, 85
Appreciation, expression of, 54, 55, 86, 87
Approach-avoidance situation, 77
Argumentativeness, 24
Arrogance, 24
Assertion, *see* Assertive behavior, Assertiveness, *and* Positive assertion
Assertive behavior, vii–viii, 7, 12–13, 17–18, 27–29, 33–47, 64–100
   components of, 12–13
   maintaining, 99–100
   nonverbal, 49, 61–63, 67
   situational determinants of, 86–88

Assertive behavior (continued)
   verbal, 48, 49–61, 64–66
Assertive Behavior Checklist, 33, 34–36
Assertive Behavior Record Form, 33, 37–41, 64, 111–116
   use of, 88–89
Assertive personality structure, 11–12
Assertive training, vii–viii, 4
   practical applications of, 31–99
   preparation for, 33–47
   rise of, 11–13
Assertiveness (*see also* Assertive behavior)
   as adaptive behavior, 15, 17–19, 20, 24
   defined, 15
   stimulus-specific theory of, 88
Attention, 81
Attentional process, 70
Audiotapes, use of, in assertive training, 64, 83–85
Audiovisual feedback, 64, 67, 83–85
Autonomic nervous system, 7

Bandura, A., 70, 76, 89, 101
Bastein, S., 101
Behavior (*see also* Assertive behavior, Nonassertive behavior, Operant behavior, *and* Respondent behavior)
   adaptive versus unadaptive, 15–29
   evaluating, 43–47
   nonverbal, 49, 61–63, 87
   therapy, vii, 4, 10–13
   verbal, 48, 49–61, 64–66
Behavioral analysis, 33, 34–43
Behavioral Assertiveness Test, 84
Behavioral procedures, 64–90

Behavioral rater, 67
Behavioral rehearsal, 64, 67–69, 89, 95
    with modeling and coaching, 73–77
    and taped feedback, 84–85
Bellack, A. S., 102
Bergin, A. E., 89, 101
Blanchard, E. B., 86, 87, 101
Body movement, 49, 62, 68

Calhoun, K. S., 47, 101
Calmness, 85
Central nervous system, 7
Ciminero, A. R., 47, 101
Coaching, 83
    behavioral rehearsal and, 73–77
Cognitive restructuring, 33–34, 45–47,
    57
Combativeness, 24
Commendatory assertion, 54
Communication
    breakdown, 94, 95
    facial, 63
Compliments
    accepting, 48, 57, 66
    giving, 48, 55
Conciliation, 98
Conditioning, 20
    classical, 12
    covert, 64, 77–80
    operant, 8–10
Conflict resolution, 4, 10
Confrontation, 16, 24, 92, 95
Constipation, 20
Continuous reinforcement, 9
Conversation
    initiating, 48, 50
    maintaining, 48, 50–51
    terminating, 48, 59
Covert conditioning, 64, 77–80
Covert modeling, 64, 77, 78–80
Covert rehearsal, 73–76
Covert reinforcement, 64, 77
Covert sensitization, 64, 77–78
Cowardice, 25
Crisis situation, 91, 92, 98
Cultural relativity, 15, 16, 17
Cursing, 53

Dawley, H. H., Jr., 90, 103, 105n
Defensiveness, 24

Deibert, A. N., 4, 101
Delo, J. S., 101
Dependent variable, 9–10
Depression, 99
Diplomacy, 55
Disagreement, 57, 65–66
Disappointment, 86
Discomfort, 98, 100
Displeasure, 86
Distance, and interaction, 49, 62, 67
Domineeringness, 24
Drive, 10
Dropping out, 16

Eisenson, J., 101
Eisler, R. M., 13, 71, 72, 81, 83, 84, 86,
    87, 88, 101, 102
Eliciting stimulus, 7, 10
Ellis, A., 24, 101
Emmons, M. L., 21, 101
Emotional ties, shallow, 16, 24
Emotions, expressing, 48, 52–53, 86
    (see also Feelings)
Empathy, 48, 54, 55, 56
Excitation, 20
Excitatory personality structure, 11–
    12
Exercises
    relaxation, 85, 105–110
    voice, 60–61
Explanation, asking for, 48, 58, 66
Extinction, 9, 82
Eye contact, 49, 61, 62, 66, 67, 87

Facial expression, 67
Facial talk, 49, 63
Facilitation, 13
Fear, 7, 18, 20, 59, 62, 70, 85, 99
    neurotic, 12
Feedback, 33, 44, 63, 76
    audiovisual, 64, 67, 83–85
    research on, 69–70
Feelings, positive, 48, 54–56 (see also
    Emotions)
Fluency, 48, 61, 67, 87
Ford, H., 4, 101
Friedman, P. H., 83, 84, 101
Frustration, 21, 22, 52
Fury, 24

Galassi, J. P., 85, 101
Galassi, M. D., 85, 101
Garfield, 89, 101
Gay, M. L., 101
General, D., 90, 103, 105n
Guilt, 7, 16, 20, 22, 45, 61, 91, 92–93, 100

Habit, 10
Habituation, 13
Harmon, A. J., 5, 101
Headache, 20
Hersen, M., 13, 71, 72, 81, 83, 84, 86, 87, 101, 102
Hollandsworth, J. G., 101
Homework, 83
Homosexuality, 16
Honesty, emotional, 48, 53–54
Hostile assertion, 54, 55, 86
Hostility, 3, 24, 52, 92, 95, 99, 100
Hypertension, 85

Idiosyncratic view, 15, 16, 17
Imagery, 77, 79
Independent variables, 10
Indiscriminate agreement, 57
Information giving, 83
Inhibition, 18, 20, 70, 99
    excessive, 16
Inhibitory, 20–21 22
Insecurity, 61, 62
Insight, 3
Insomnia, 20
Intermittent reinforcement, 9
Interpersonal understanding, 3
Intrapsychic conflict, 3

Jacobson, E., 85, 102
Johnson, M. B., 71–72, 102
Justification, 58, 66

Kanfer, F. H., 80, 102
Karoly, P., 80, 102
Kazdin, A. E., 78, 79, 102

Laws, D. R. 13, 102
Lazarus, A. A., 12, 13, 43, 44, 46, 54, 68, 69, 102, 105n

Learning, 4, 10, 16, 19
Lillesand, D. B., 73, 74, 75, 83, 84, 102
Listening, 56
Litz, M. C., 85, 101
Loosening up, 105
Loudness, 60–61, 67, 87

McFall, R. M., 69, 73, 74, 75, 83, 84, 102
MacPherson, E. L., 82, 102
Mahoney, M. J., 80–81, 90, 103
Malott, R., 13, 102, 103
Marston, A. R., 69, 73, 83, 84, 102
Masters, J. C., 89, 102
Meekness, 61
Miller, P. M., 13, 71, 72, 81, 83, 84, 86, 87, 101, 102
Minorities, and self-assertion, 20
Misperception, 45
Modeling, 64, 68, 70–77
    audio, 75, 76
    behavioral rehearsal and, 73–77
    covert, 78–80
    versus instruction, 76
    and taped feedback, 84–85
Modesty, 18, 56
Motivational process, 70
Motor act, 53
Motoric reproduction process, 70
Muscle group, 105

Negative reinforcer, 9, 80
Negative trait, 3
Neurotic fear, 12
Nonassertive behavior (*see also* Nonassertiveness)
    nonverbal, 49, 61–63
    verbal, 48, 49–61
Nonassertiveness, xv–xvi, 19–23
    defined, 16
    general, 21–23
    situational, 21–23
    as unadaptive behavior, 15, 17–19
Nonverbal behavior, 49, 61–63, 87

Operant behavior, 6, 7–8
Operant conditioning, 8–10
Oppositionalism, 24
Ostracism, 24

Outside observer, 33, 44, 99
Overassertiveness, 24
Overt rehearsal, 73–76

Paralinguistic component, 67
Passive disagreement, 57, 65–66
Pavlov, I. P., 20
Personality, 4
Pinkston, S. G., 71–72, 102
Positive asserton, 55, 86–88
Positive feelings, 48, 54–56
Positive reinforcer, 9, 80
Posture, 49, 61, 62, 67
Praise, 86, 87
Psychoanalysis, 10, 11
Psychophysiological disorder, 20
Psychosomatic disorder, 20
Psychotherapy, 3, 4, 10, 11, 83
Punishment, 9, 20
  self-, 80

Rachman, S., 14, 102
Rathus, S. A., 42, 65, 66n, 85, 102
Rathus Assertiveness Schedule (RAS),
  33, 42–43, 66
Reality testing, 33, 44–45
Refusal, 48, 58–59, 74
Regret, 45
Rehabilitation, 13
Rehearsal
  behavioral, 64, 67–69, 73–77, 89, 95
  covert, 73–76
  overt, 73–76
Reinforcement
  continuous, 9
  covert, 64, 77
  intermittent, 9
  nonverbal, 81
  process, 70, 71
  self-, 54, 80, 81
  uses of, 80–82
  verbal, 81
Reinforcer, 20
  negative, 9, 80
  positive, 9, 80
Rejection, risk of, 55
Relaxation, 68
  exercises, 85, 105–110
  and tension, 105–110
  training, 64, 85
Release, 53

Remorse, 16, 99
Requests, making, 48, 58
Resentment, 12, 22, 45, 52
Respect, 81
Respondent behavior, 6, 7–8, 10
Retention process, 70
Reticence, 45
Rights, 51
Rimm, D. C., 89, 102
Ritterby, K., 13, 102
Role playing, 64, 67, 68, 69–70, 82, 95

Salter, A., 11, 12, 14, 16, 20, 21, 22,
  53, 54, 56, 63, 65n, 102
Screaming, 53
Self-concept, 23
Self-confidence, 56, 81
Self-control, 99
Self-denial, 70
Self-esteem, 99, 100
Self-evaluation, 43–47, 80
Self-monitoring, 80
Self-punishment, 80
Self-regulation, 80
Self-reinforcement, 80, 81
Self-reward, 80, 81
Sensitization, covert, 64, 77–78
Serber, M., 13, 67, 72, 84, 102
Sex role, 20
Shame, 22
Shyness, 56
Significance, in statistics, 66n
Significant others, 81
  feedback from, 33
  and role playing, 68
Situational aggressiveness, 25–29
Situational determinants, of assertive
  behavior, 86–88
Smiling, 63, 87
  hostility, 94
Social obligations, 46
Sorrow, 45
Speech fluency, 48, 61
Spontaneity, 21, 87
Stimuli, 9
Stimulus, eliciting, 7, 10
Stimulus-specific theory, 88
Success, 16

Tact, 55, 59

Talk
  assertive, 65
  extemporaneous, 48, 51–52
  facial, 49
  feeling, 48, 53–54, 65
  greeting, 48, 56, 65
  about oneself, 48, 56–57, 66
Tape recorder, use of, in assertive
        training, 60, 61, 64, 68, 69, 83–85
Tension, and relaxation, 105–110
Tharp, R. G., 90, 103
Therapist, 33, 44, 83, 89, 99, 100
Thoresen, C. E., 80–81, 90, 103
Timidity, 61, 62
Training tape, 73
Tranquility, 85
Troubleshooting, 91–100
Twentyman, C. T., 74, 75, 76, 102

Understanding, 54, 55
  interpersonal, 3
Urban, H., 4, 101

Variables, 9–10
Verbal behavior, 48, 49–61
Verbal skills, 64, 65–66
Videotapes, use of, in assertive
        training, 64, 71, 72, 73, 83–85, 88
Violence, 24
Voice, 48, 51, 68
  exercises, 60–61
  volume, 60–61, 67, 87

Watson, D. L., 90, 103
Wenrich, W. W., 14, 90, 103, 105n
Whaley, D., 13, 14, 102, 103
Wolf, E. L., 13, 102
Wolpe, J., 12, 14, 45, 54, 67, 68n, 80,
        86, 103, 105n
Women, and self-assertion, 20